# The Cherokees

BIBLIOGRAPHICAL SERIES
*The Newberry Library Center
for the History of the American Indian*

*General Editor*
Francis Jennings

*The Center Is Supported by Grants from*

The National Endowment for the Humanities
The Ford Foundation
The W. Clement and Jessie V. Stone Foundation
The Woods Charitable Fund, Inc.

# The Cherokees

*A Critical Bibliography*

RAYMOND D. FOGELSON

Published for the Newberry Library
*Indiana University Press*
BLOOMINGTON AND LONDON

Copyright © 1978 by Indiana University Press
All rights reserved

No part of this book may be reproduced or utilized in any form or by any means, electronic or mechanical, including photocopying and recording, or by any information storage and retrieval system, without permission in writing from the publisher. The Association of American University Presses' Resolution on Permissions constitutes the only exception to this prohibition.

Manufactured in the United States of America

```
Library of Congress Cataloging in Publication Data
Fogelson, Raymond D
  The Cherokees, a critical bibliography.
  (Bibliographical series)
  Includes index.
  1. Cherokee Indians--Bibliography.  I. Title.
Z1210.C46F64    [E99.C5]    016.970'.004'97    78-3254
ISBN 0-253-31346-5    1 2 3 4 5 82 81 80 79. 78
```

## CONTENTS

| | |
|---|---|
| The Editor to the Reader | vii |
| Recommended Works | 1 |
| Bibliographical Essay | |
|     Introduction | 3 |
|     Basic Reference Works | 6 |
|     General Sources on the Cherokees | 8 |
|     Prehistory and Archeology | 10 |
|     The Colonial Period | 11 |
|     The Revolution and Its Aftermath | 15 |
|     Regeneration | 17 |
|     Removal | 19 |
|     Cherokees in the West | 21 |
|     The Eastern Cherokees | 25 |
|     Language | 28 |
|     Ecology, Natural History, and Material Culture | 31 |
|     Social Organization | 33 |
|     World View, Religion, and Medicine | 35 |
|     Personality and Biography | 41 |
| Alphabetical List and Index | 44 |

## THE EDITOR TO THE READER

A massive literature exists for the history and culture of American Indians, but the quality of that literature is very uneven. At its best it compares well with the finest scholarship and most interesting reading to be found anywhere. At its worst it may take the form of malicious fabrication. Sometimes well-intentioned writers give false impressions of reality either because of their own limitations of mind or because they lack adequate information. The consequence is a kind of chaos through which advanced scholars as well as new students must warily pick their way. It is, after all, a history of hundreds, if not thousands, of human communities spread over an entire continent and enduring through millennia of pre-Columbian years as well as the five centuries that Europeans have documented since 1492. That is not a small amount of history.

Often, however, historians have been so concerned with the affairs of European colonies or the United States that they have almost omitted Indians from their own history. There is a way of writing "frontier history" and the "history of Indian-White relations" that often focuses so narrowly upon the intentions and desires of Euro-Americans as to treat Native Americans as though they were merely natural parts of the landscape, like forests or mountains or wild animals — obstacles to "progress" or "civilization." One of the major purposes of the Newberry Library's Center for the History of the American Indian is to modify that narrow conception; to put Indians properly back into the central role in their own history and into the history of the United States of America as well — as participants in, rather than obstacles to, the creation of American society and culture.

The series of bibliographies of which this book is one part is intended as a guide to reliable sources and studies in particular fields of the general literature. Some of these are devoted to culture areas; others treat selected individual tribes; and a third group speaks to significant contemporary and historical issues.

The present book deals with one of the most extensively studied North American tribes. It is not surprising that the literature about Cherokees should be so vast, considering their eventful history. During the years of imperial struggle between France and Britain for control of the continent, the Cherokees played a critical role on the southern frontier, as they did again during the American War for Independence. They adopted Euro-American methods of farming, built clapboard houses, kept slaves, invented a syllabary for recording their language, and published a newspaper. Though they thus transformed themselves into a "civilized tribe," most of them were forced to take the "Trail of Tears" to the west, and now they are scattered from the Atlantic coast to the Pacific. The literature is as varied, and ranges as widely, as their history. Only such a master scholar as Professor Fogelson could guide the student through its complexities.

This work is designed in a format, standard for the series, intended to be useful to both beginning students and advanced scholars. It has two main parts: the essay (conveniently organized by subheadings) and an alphabetical list of all works cited. All citations in the essay are directly keyed, by means of bracketed numbers, to the more complete publication data in the list; and each item in the list carries a cross-reference to the page number where it is mentioned in the essay. In addition, the series incorporates several information-at-a-glance features. Among them are two sets of recommended titles: a list of five works recommended for the beginner and a group of volumes that constitute a basic library collection in the field. The large, complete list also uses asterisks to denote works suitable for secondary school students. This apparatus has been built in because the bibliographical essay, in a form familiar to scholars, could prove fairly hard going for beginners, who may wish to put it aside until they have gained sufficient background from introductory materials. Such students should come back to the essay eventually, however, because it surveys a vast sweep of information about a great variety of persons, places, communities, and events.

There is variety also in the kinds of sources because these critical bibliographies support the study of ethnohistory. Unlike older, more narrow disciplines, ethnohistory embraces the entire culture of a people; it demands contributions from a wide range of source materials. Not the least of these in the history of American Indians are their own music, crafts, linguistics, and oral traditions. Whenever possible, the authors have included such sources as well as those associated with politics, economics, geography, and so on. It will be recognized that the variety of relevant sources will change with the nature of the topic discussed.

In the last analysis this work, like all other bibliographical devices, is a tool. Each author is an expert who knows the literature and advises what source is most helpful for which purpose, but students must use this help according to their individual purposes and capacities. Many ways suggest themselves. The decision is the reader's own.

## RECOMMENDED WORKS

### For the Beginner

[28]   Brown, John P., *Old Frontiers.*

[31]   Burt, Jesse, and Robert Ferguson, *Indians of the Southeast, Then and Now.*

[35]   Carter, Samuel, III, *Cherokee Sunset: A Nation Betrayed.*

[225]  Mooney, James, "Myths of the Cherokees."

[345]  Woodward, Grace Steele, *The Cherokees.*

### For a Basic Library Collection

[3]    Adair, James, *History of the American Indians.*

[47]   Corkran, David H., *Cherokee Frontier: Conflict and Survival.*

[66]   Debo, Angie, *And Still the Waters Run.*

[80]   Fenton, William N., and John Gulick, eds. *Symposium on Cherokee and Iroquois Culture.*

[108]  Gearing, Frederick O., *Priests and Warriors: Social Structure for Cherokee Politics in the 18th Century.*

[109]  Gilbert, William H. Jr., *The Eastern Cherokees.*

[115]   Goodwin, Gary C., *Cherokees in Transition: A Study of Changing Culture and Environment prior to 1775.*

[153]   Hudson, Charles, *The Southeastern Indians.*

[170]   Kilpatrick, Jack F., and Anna G., eds. *The Shadow of Sequoyah: Social Documents of the Cherokees, 1862–1964.*

[209]   Malone, Henry T., *Cherokees of the Old South.*

[226]   Mooney, James, and Frans M. Olbrechts, *The Swimmer Manuscript: Cherokee Sacred Formulas and Medicinal Prescriptions.*

[264]   Royce, Charles C., "The Cherokee Nation of Indians: A Narrative of Their Official Relations with the Colonial and Federal Governments."

[281]   Speck, Frank G., and Leonard Broom, *Cherokee Dance and Drama.*

[289]   Strickland, Rennard, *Fire and the Spirits: Cherokee Law from Clan to Court.*

[326]   Wilkins, Thurman, *Cherokee Tragedy: The Story of the Ridge Family and the Decimation of a People.*

# BIBLIOGRAPHICAL ESSAY

## Introduction

With the possible exception of the Northern Iroquois and the Navajos, probably more has been written about the Cherokees than any other Native American group. They were a dominant tribe in the Southeast, experienced an eventful history tempered by tragedy and triumph, and continue today as a viable and significant people. The voluminous literature on the Cherokees is multifaceted and uneven. Certain topics, such as the Cherokee Removal, or poetry and fiction inspired by Cherokee themes, could easily merit separate bibliographic treatment. Other topics, however, are woefully underrepresented in the published literature: for example, native accounts of the "Trail of Tears," or hard data on early Cherokee town size and marriage patterns.

Over the past two decades I have accumulated, without concerted search, several thousand references to the Cherokees. In preparing this bibliography I located over a thousand more citations. Reducing references to a number suitable to the format and intention of this bibliographic series proved an arduous task. The

> I want to acknowledge the assistance and encouragement of several colleagues who knowingly or unknowingly helped bring this project to fruition: Paul Kutsche, who abetted my early interest in Cherokee bibliography; Janet Jordan and Willard Walker, who shared with me their unpublished Cherokee bibliography; Charlotte Heth and William Sturtevant, who supplied many stray references; Gary Goodwin and Robert Brightman, two students who proved to be assiduous bibliographers; and Susan Hopkins and Susan Martich, who proved to be adept graphologists.

problem might have been simplified somewhat had I decided to compile either an anthropological or a historical bibliography on the Cherokees. But since I am an anthropologist with historical interests (what used to be called an ethnologist), and since I am firmly convinced that the two perspectives must be combined to produce a satisfactory understanding of Cherokee culture, I have selected sources from both history and anthropology.

Several criteria guided my choices for inclusion and exclusion. In general, I favored major monographs rather than articles by the same author on similar or related topics. Topical surveys, which might include some comparative material on the Cherokees along with other American Indians, were usually avoided. Highly specific sources that I deemed of limited interest and sources that unduly strained my categorical imperatives were allowed to flow freely through my net. I tended to select newer and more comprehensive references, with the expectation that earlier and more fragmentary sources would be cited therein. Many key works on the Cherokees have been issued in multiple editions; here my selection was influenced by the scholarly worth of the introductions and annotations and by accessibility. I have made no effort to list all editions of a particular work.

My biggest regret was the impossibility of including Cherokee publications intended primarily for Cherokee readers. Many Cherokees became literate in English by the first decades of the nineteenth century, and soon thereafter Sequoyah devised a syllabary enabling native Cherokee-speakers to read and write their own language. As a result many important types of literature appeared, including newspapers, biblical translations, religious and educational tracts, legal statutes, political memorials and petitions, and other matters of concern to the Cherokee population.

I have also neglected most official government documents: colonial papers, treaties, reports to the Commissioner of Indian Affairs, congressional reports, American state papers, census reports, and similar types of material. The dedicated scholar can find specialized guides to this labyrinthine literature.

Untold riches of Cherokee material are preserved in manuscript form. John Alden [4] has surveyed eighteenth-century Cherokee archives, and William Jones [156] has provided a guide to material on the Five Civilized Tribes in the University of Oklahoma Library. A valuable listing of manuscript and rare materials held by the Thomas Gilcrease Institute has been compiled by Lester Hargrett [130]. Partial listings of important manuscript collections appear in works by Corkran [47], Cotterill [51], Strickland [289], Wilkins [326], and Woodward [345]. A list of archival centers containing significant Cherokee manuscript material might minimally include the following: the American Philosophical Society Library, the Newberry Library, the National Anthropological Archives of the Smithsonian Institution, Duke University Library, University of North Carolina Library, Western Carolina University Library, the Houghton Library at Harvard, the Clements Library at the University of Michigan, the Cherokee Collection at Northeastern Oklahoma College, the McFarlan Library at the University of Tulsa, the Oklahoma Historical Society, the South Carolina Historical Society, the Tennessee State Library and Archives, the North Carolina State Department of Archives and History, the Georgia Department of Archives and History, the Museum of the Cherokee Indian in Cherokee, North Carolina, and the Cherokee National Historical Society in Tahlequah, Oklahoma. A set of recent oral history transcripts is deposited at the Florida State Museum in Gainesville.

Much essential Cherokee material can be found in the pages of unpublished masters' theses and doctoral dissertations. Frederick and Alice Dockstader have compiled an excellent guide [72] to these underutilized materials; this reference work lists 160 specifically Cherokee entries through 1970, and several more can be found under other categories. However, academic interest in the Cherokees continues apace, and many important dissertations have been produced since 1970.

**Basic Reference Works**

John R. Swanton's *Indians of the Southeastern United States* [291] is the most comprehensive work on the Southeastern culture area. Despite its many virtues, this work slights the Cherokees, since Swanton considered them late immigrants into the Southeast and marginal to the Southeastern cultural core; thus treatment of the

Cherokees in his magnum opus is scanty. More recent linguistic [207], archeological [39], and ethnological [87] opinion argues for longer Cherokee residence in the Southeast and closer integration into the general Southeastern culture pattern. This view is reflected in the prominent position given to the Cherokees in Charles Hudson's *The Southeastern Indians* [153], the best recent synthesis of the area, and Jesse Burt and Robert Ferguson's *Indians of the Southeast, Then and Now* [31], a less scholarly work, but one filled with useful information.

The extensive Murdock and O'Leary bibliography [230] serves well as the logical first step in searching out Cherokee ethnographic references through 1972. This can be usefully supplemented by recourse to the earlier two-volume *Anthropological Bibliography of the Eastern Seaboard* [263, 122], issued by the Eastern States Archaeological Federation; this reference work includes more archeological references as well as a sampling of historical and ethnological sources. Donald Ball has recently produced *A Bibliography on Tennessee Anthropology* [10], which again is weighted toward archeology but contains numerous historical and ethnographic citations, and David Phelps has edited a comparable bibliography for North Carolina [244].

The premier reference for historical bibliography is Francis P. Prucha's remarkable *Bibliographic Guide to the History of Indian-White Relations in the United States* [250]. Prucha has a separate Cherokee section, and the many other Cherokee references included under his various topical headings can be located through his careful index. The Butterfield, Washburn, and Fenton bibliography [79] is a bit dated but still useful, particularly for Fenton's essay on needs and opportunities for studying Indian-White relations. T. D. Clark's three-volume bibliography *Travels in the Old South* [37] contains references to obscure and famous travelers who wrote about their visits to the Cherokee country.

Many regional journals consistently include historical articles on the Cherokees. Prominent among these are: *The Chronicles of Oklahoma, The North Carolina Historical Review, East Tennessee Historical Society Publications, The Tennessee Historical Quarterly, Early Georgia,* and *The Georgia Historical Quarterly.* Finally, a *Journal of Cherokee Studies* has recently been launched under the skilled editorship of Duane King; this medium should serve as a prime source for Cherokee studies for years to come.

### General Sources on the Cherokees

James Mooney's durable "Myths of the Cherokees" [225] still stands alone as the best introduction to Cherokee history and ethnology. Mooney was not only a gifted ethnohistorian but a fieldworker of rare talent and ingenuity as well. His sketch of Cherokee history needs only minor revision today and has recently been reprinted in paperback. Mooney's historical treatment is enhanced with informant recollections, and as a result the later periods of Eastern Cherokee history are superb, though Western Cherokee history is less detailed since Mooney spent little time there [cf. 19]. His collection of myths is exceptional for its time, and the rich lode of ethnological and linguistic material contained in the formidable footnotes and glossaries is still being productively mined by modern scholars. One testimony to the value of Mooney's myth collection is the frequency with which certain myths have been expropriated, often without acknowledgment, in popular and children's works about Indians.

Two useful general accounts of the Cherokees are Marian Starkey's *The Cherokee Nation* [284] and Grace Woodward's *The Cherokees* [345]. Starkey incorporated considerable archival material from the American Board of Commissioners for Foreign Missions, and her treatment is particularly strong for the immediate pre-Removal period. Woodward's work involved extensive library research but is too often ethnologically naive and overemphasizes an orthogenetic rise to "civilization." Irwin Peithman's *Red Men of Fire* [242] is somewhat thin in data and has sensationalist overtones, yet the major events of Cherokee history are covered. Fairly good, brief general treatments of the Cherokees can be found in the relevant chapters of the books by Chapman Milling [218], Douglas Rights [257-258], and T. M. N. Lewis and Madeleine Kneberg [200]. The recent volume in the Indian Tribal Series on the Cherokees, by Earl Boyd Pierce and Rennard Strickland [247], suffers from unrelenting "boosterism." Colonial and federal treaty relations are documented and commented upon in Charles C. Royce's still-useful *The Cherokee Nation of Indians* [264].

**Prehistory and Archeology**

Cherokee prehistoric origins are just now coming into focus as a result of recent research. Much nineteenth-century speculation that tried to link the historic Cherokees with the legendary mound-builders is engagingly summarized by Robert Silverberg [272]. Scientific archeological work for the first half of the present century was generally premised on the notion of late Cherokee entry into the Southeast; as a result, very little time depth was posited for Cherokee remains. A change of opinion, favoring an *in situ* development of Cherokee culture, is signaled by Joffre Coe's paper in 1961 [39]. Roy Dickens and Bennie Keel, two younger archeologists formerly associated with Coe, have each produced major monographs [71, 157] that convincingly link the historical Cherokees with prehistoric cultural traditions. These two monographs, though based on different bodies of excavated data, complement each other and together compose the most up-to-date analyses of Cherokee origins.

Several useful site reports of historic Cherokee towns have been published. These include Peachtree [271], Hiwassee Island [198], Settico [197], Estatoe [158], Chauga [159], New Echota [61], and several sites in the Tellico Reservoir area [195, 113, 114]. William Sears [270] has offered an interpretation of eighteenth-century Creek and Cherokee culture from an archeological perspective, and David Halley [126] has written a general archeological survey of European-Indian contact in the Southeast.

Hiram Wilburn [323, 324] has discussed one of the more famous petroglyphs attributed to the Cherokees, and David Corkran [46] speculates about Cherokee origins on the basis of two early manuscript fragments.

**The Colonial Period**

The colonial period encompasses initial European contact with the Cherokees through the onset of the American Revolution. For the Cherokees this period was marked by population reduction resulting from disease and warfare, consolidation of loosely affiliated autonomous towns into a centralized polity, increased dependency on European trade goods, and ultimate military subjugation.

The first Europeans to make contact with the Cherokees were the Spaniards. There is some uncertainty whether de Soto's 1539–40 *entrada* into the Southeast ventured into what was then Cherokee country. At most, only a few villages were reached, but the Cherokees would have felt the impact of de Soto's invasion through intermediate groups. Later Spanish expeditions led by Pardo and Boyano definitely reached the Cherokees [225]. Alvord and Bidgood [7] summarize the first Trans-Allegheny explorations by Virginians that eventuated in permanent English contact. The primary motives for early English exploration were the establishment of trade and military alliances; only later did land acquisition become an obsession. The best general treatment of the early colonial period is Verner Crane's *The Southern Frontier: 1670–1732* [52]. Briefer accounts of the trade are Franklin [103-104], Rights

[257], Vassar [300], and Rothrock [262].

Without doubt the most valuable eighteenth-century treatise on the Southern Indians is James Adair's *History of the American Indians* [3]. Adair was a trader with over thirty years' residence among the Cherokees and Chickasaws. He combined an acute eye and general sympathy for the Indians with shrewd Scottish pragmatism. It is sometimes difficult to determine the specific tribes he is referring to in general ethnographic sections of the book, although he does have a special chapter on the Cherokees, dealing primarily with political affairs. Adair was a firm advocate of the Hebraic origin of the Indians and advanced detailed arguments in support of this hypothesis. Later scholars have felt that this bias makes some of his information suspect, but a more generous evaluation would maintain that Adair's "ethnological hypothesis" forced cultural comparisons with the ancient Hebrews and thereby led him to present details of Indian customs, particularly features of social organization and religion, that might otherwise have gone unrecorded.

Other important firsthand accounts with rich data are the *Report* of DeBrahm, which has recently been lavishly edited by Louis DeVorsey, Jr. [68], the *Memoirs of Lieutenant Henry Timberlake* [327], and the famous *Travels* [15] and subsequent "Observations of the Creek and Cherokee Indians" [14] by William Bartram. DeBrahm was a military architect who was intellectually curious about the Cherokees. Timberlake was a soldier whose spirited description is based on a diplomatic visit to the Overhills Cherokee after the French and Indian War and on his trip to London with a small Cherokee embassy. Bartram was a skilled naturalist, but his stay among the Cherokees was all too brief, and his reportage occasionally lapses into romanticism (indeed, his book was widely read in its day and inspired many of the great English poets of the romantic movement). The best edition of Bartram is by Francis Harper and is a model of scholarship.

Many briefer primary accounts deserve mention. David Corkran has discovered and edited one of the earliest extended descriptions of the Cherokees, Alexander Longe's early eighteenth century "Postscript" [48]. Longe was a trader and has interesting observations on Cherokee religion. "Relations of Facts," by another early trader, Ludovick Grant [116], recounts the mercurial diplomatic embassy of Sir Alexander Cumming in 1730. Cumming succeeded in bringing a delegation of Cherokees to England, where they swore allegiance to the king and proved to be the sensation of the London social season, as documented by Carolyn Foreman [91]. The career of Christian Gottlieb Priber, who briefly organized the Cherokees into a socialist utopian state in 1736, is discussed by Strickland [288] and Mellon [215]. Unfortunately, none of Priber's own writings survived his imprisonment. An unsuccessful Presbyterian missionary left a brief account for 1757–59 [329]. Samuel Cole Williams has edited a valuable collection of *Early Travels in the Tennessee Country, 1540–1800* [328], which collates some of the above-mentioned accounts as well as several others. Williams has also written a narrative history, *Dawn of Tennessee Valley and Tennessee History* [330], which helps fill in the period between Crane's *Southern Frontier* and the Revolution; some of this intervening period is also covered in Archibald Henderson's *Conquest of the Old Southwest* [136]. J. Ralph Randolph's *British Travelers among the Southern Indians, 1660–1763* [254] is a well-written secondary source.

Many excellent works recount the political maneuvering and strife that began in the mid-eighteenth century and culminated in the American Revolution. Corkran's *The Cherokee Frontier: Conflict and Survival, 1740–1762* [47] and his later *The Carolina Indian Frontier* [49] are essential sources for understanding this period. Robinson's essay on Virginia and the Cherokees [259] also clarifies certain matters. Wilbur Jacobs's edition of the *Edmond Atkins Report and Plan of 1755* [154] and Philip Hamer's article "Anglo-French Rivalry in the Cherokee Country, 1754–1757" [128] document the crises leading to the French and Indian War in the Southeast. The war itself, including the massacre at Fort Loudoun, is covered in John P. Brown's *Old Frontiers* [28] and in another article by Hamer [129]. John Alden's book *John Stuart and the Southern Colonial Frontier* [5] documents the problems of British management of Indian affairs in attempting to mediate the growing strife between the colonial settlers and the increasingly engulfed Cherokees. DeVorsey provides a fine account of *The Indian Boundary in the Southern Colonies, 1763–*

*1775* [69], in which his skills as an historical geographer are much in evidence.

Judge John Haywood's *The Natural and Aboriginal History of Tennessee,* first published in 1823, deserves special comment. Haywood was a pioneer archeologist, but his book also provides considerable information on traditional Cherokee institutions and customs; the Rothrock edition is well annotated [133].

Out of the colonial experience came more precise knowledge of Southeastern geography. Some of this development can be traced through William Cumming's collection *The Southeast in Early Maps* [54] and in a subsequent article [55]. A complementary image of the Southeastern landscape can be gleaned from William Myer's "Indian Trails of the Southeast" [231].

## The Revolution and Its Aftermath

The American Revolution was not a revolution for the Cherokees, but rather a series of diplomatic and military defeats in which they once more were losing pawns on an international gaming board. With France effectively out of the contest for New World empire, the Cherokees supported the British in a final effort to checkmate the steadily mounting pressure of the colonial settlers. Early in the war Cherokee villages were devastated by American armies, treaties were signed, and much land was ceded. Dissident Cherokees retreated to the Chickamauga settlements, near present-day Chattanooga, and with Spanish assistance continued hostilities until 1792.

James O'Donnell's book *Southern Indians in the American Revolution* [233] provides the best overview of those events. Williams offers an informative synopsis, *Tennessee during the Revolutionary War* [331], and Duane King has written a balanced assessment of the Cherokee situation in 1776 [178]. Henderson presents details on the 1777 Treaty of Long Island of Holston [137]. Cherokee-American relations from 1776 to 1791 are reviewed by Randolph Downes [74], and the testimony of General Joseph Martin, an active participant in these events, has been edited by Meriwether [217]. Spain's continuing influence in the affairs of this period is discussed by Arthur Whitaker [317].

Several early regional historians present primary data on the Revolution and subsequent events; much of their information comes from personal reminiscences and oral tradition. The most important of these sources are A. J. Pickett [246], J. G. H. Ramsey [253], G. R. Gilmer [112], A. W. Putnam [252], and J. H. Logan [206]. There is a predictable tendency in these histories to glorify the heroism of ancestors and to portray the Cherokees as irredeemable savages destined for extinction.

No really satisfactory account of the Chickamaugans and their continuing resistance to the Americans exists. Many Chickamauga survivors became the first Cherokee emigrants to the West. Some basic information is provided in Mooney [225] and Brown [28], but a more interpretive analysis is needed.

**Regeneration**

The story of the Cherokee renaissance during the first third of the nineteenth century has been told and retold. The achievements of the Cherokees in elevating themselves to the status of a "civilized" tribe, as measured by prosperous plantations, Christianity, and literacy, highlight most general treatments of the Cherokees; these achievements lend dramatic poignancy to the subsequent wrenching tragedy of Removal. Henry T. Malone's *Cherokees of the Old South* [209] is an important source for the period. Malone not only chronicles events but also describes the development of Cherokee social institutions in relation to general Southern culture of the period.

Protestant missionaries were a significant instrument in fulfilling the plans of Washington and Jefferson to transform the Cherokees into a nation of settled agrarians, espousing Christian virtues and valuing education. Robert Berkhofer's *Salvation and the Savage* [21] is an insightful analysis that sets the historical context and reports the results of the missionary endeavor. The Moravians were the first missionary group to establish schools and gain a foothold among the Cherokees. Edmund Schwarze [269] presents a general history of Moravian missions among the Southeastern Indians. The diaries of these Moravian missionaries remain mostly untranslated in Moravian archives, but the 1799 report of Steiner and von Schweinitz is available in Williams [328], and De Baillou [65] offers translated excerpts from 1800–1804 diaries.

The most influential missionaries among the pre-Removal Cherokees were those associated with the American Board of Commissioners for Foreign Missions. Robert Walker [308] has contributed a book-length history of the Brainerd Mission, and Starkey's *Cherokee Nation* [284] is liberally sprinkled with material from the ABCFM archives. Samuel A. Worcester, an activist missionary who began his work with the Cherokees in the 1820s and continued his labors after Removal to the Indian Territory, is the subject of a biography by Althea Bass [16]. More work needs to be done with the ABCFM papers, particularly with the unpublished diaries and papers of the scholar-missionary Daniel S. Butrick.

James Moffitt has written "Early Baptist Missionary Work among the Cherokees" [219], and Mary Peacock has reviewed "Methodist Mission Work among the Cherokee Indians before the Removal" [241]. These two denominations came to have an enduring influence on later Cherokee religious life. The missionaries encountered some resistance among culturally conservative Cherokees, and McLoughlin documents "Cherokee Anti-Missionary Sentiment, 1824–1828" [214].

The availability of black slave labor provided the infrastructure of much Cherokee "social advancement" and "civilization" during this period. The first of Annie Heloise Abel's three-volume work *Slaveholding Indians* [2] continues to be a useful source on slavery. Halliburton's recent *Red Over Black* [125] traces the early use of black slaves among the Cherokees and puts to rest apologetic myths that Indians treated slaves more humanely than did their white neighbors. Theda Perdue [243] convincingly shows that the idea of slavery was deeply embedded in aboriginal Cherokee society.

An important overlooked source for this period is the recently published *Journal of Major John Norton*, edited by Klinck and Talman [182]. Norton claimed to be a Cherokee by birth but was captured as a child and raised as a Mohawk. After an illustrious career as a warrior and diplomat, he visited the Cherokees in 1819 to seek out his relatives. He was hospitably received, able to acquire rudimentary conversational ability in the language, and managed to record valuable geographic and ethnographic information that would have eluded a non-Indian observer. He is particularly sensitive to Cherokee-Iroquois comparisons.

## Removal

The Removal Act of 1830 and the events leading to its implementation aroused great contemporary debate. The Removal persists as a chronic scab on the American conscience that is regularly picked by morally concerned scholars. Though all the major Southeastern Indian nations were removed westward, the case of the Cherokees commanded the most public attention and continues to engage scholars. Fascination with the Cherokee Removal can be explained by the success of the Cherokees in adapting to Euro-American modes of life, Cherokee eloquence in trying to forestall Removal through legal means, and the enormity of their suffering in their forced emigration over the infamous "Trail of Tears."

Several important recent works help put into context the political background of the Removal policy: Father Prucha's *American Indian Policy in the Formative Years* [249] is a comprehensive synthesis of general policy leading up to and including the Removal; Ronald Satz's *American Indian Policy in the Jacksonian Era* [268] sheds additional light on these issues; Michael Rogin's *Fathers and Children* [260] is a stimulating explanation of the Jacksonian mind and its social setting. Rogin combines orthodox historical documentation with radical social theory and psychoanalytic psychobiography to produce a provocative analysis.

Earlier works on the Removal that still merit attention include those by Abel [1], Foreman [99], and Walter Blumenthal [25]. Mary Young has written a valuable recent article, "Indian Removal and the Attack on Tribal Autonomy: The Cherokee Case" [346]. Other interpretations stressing legal and political aspects of the Cherokee Removal can be found in Rutland [267], Burke [30], Grindle [119], and the casebook edited by Filler and Guttmann [82]. Georgia Governor Wilson Lumpkin, a strong advocate for Cherokee Removal, states his position in a two-volume work [208]. Thurman Wilkins's well-researched *Cherokee Tragedy* [326] sympathetically portrays the tribulations of the Ridge family, who capitulated to the pressures for Removal and paid the consequences after resettlement in the Indian Territory.

The famous playwright-actor John Howard Payne spent considerable time in the Cherokee country at the height of the Removal crisis. He was a close advisor to Chief John Ross and movingly pleaded the Cherokee case. Clemens De Baillou has edited *John Howard Payne to His Countrymen* [63].

Specifics of the actual Removal are detailed by Foreman [97], Corn [50], White [320], and Burt and Ferguson [32]. Lillybridge's journal of a party of Cherokee emigrants has been published [201], and Knight [183] has assessed the general state of Cherokee society under the stress of Removal.

Many recent extended treatments of the Cherokee Removal aimed at a popular audience have appeared in print; among the more reliable and successful of these are the books by Dale Van Every [299], Glen Fleischman [83], Gloria Jahoda [155], and Samuel Carter [35].

**Cherokees in the West**

Long before the Removal exodus, groups of Cherokees voluntarily emigrated to the West. Many settled first in Arkansas and Texas. These pre-Removal emigrants are discussed by Cephas Washburn in his *Cherokees "West," 1794-1839* [314] and in Grant Foreman's *Indians and Pioneers* [95]. Additional data on the Arkansas Cherokees are available in the 1819 observations of Thomas Nuttall [232] and in two articles by Jack and Anna Kilpatrick [165], [169]. Ernest Winkler has written a lengthy article on the Texas Cherokees [334], and John Reagan describes their expulsion from East Texas [255]. A useful modern source is Mary Clarke's *Chief Bowles and the Texas Cherokees* [38]. Jack Gregory and Rennard Strickland [117] summarize Sam Houston's association with the Texas Cherokees from 1829 to 1833.

Post-Removal Cherokee readjustment is treated in Tom Holm's "Cherokee Colonization in Oklahoma" [144], Kenny Franks's "Political Intrigues in the Cherokee Nation, 1839" [105], and Foreman's *Advancing the Frontier* [93]. Morris and McReynold's *Historical Atlas of Oklahoma* [227] is helpful for locating events and boundaries.

Several general works on the Western Cherokees emphasize different historical facets: Foreman's *The Five Civilized Tribes* [98] is a standard reference; Starr's *History of the Cherokee Indians* [285] is an undigested potpourri of information, including extensive genealogies of Cherokee families in his idiosyncratic notational system; Angie Debo's *And Still the Waters Run* [66] is especially good on the graft and despoliation following the Allotment Act; Morris Wardell's *Political History of the Cherokee* [311] is a well-documented survey of Cherokee government from Removal to Oklahoma statehood in 1907; Hugh Cunningham [57] offers a brief review of Cherokee history in two continuous articles; and Peter Collier's recent *When Shall They Rest?* [40] stresses not only past but continuing injustices.

Only a sample of the large literature of informal reminiscences of life in the Indian territory can be cited here. J. M. Carselowey's *Cherokee Old Timers* [34] typifies this genre, as does Thomas Ballenger's *Around Tahlequah Council Fires* [13]. The recollections of Lucy Keys (Wahnenauhi) have been edited and published by Jack

Kilpatrick [164]. Cephus Washburn, a Presbyterian missionary who ministered to the Arkansas and post-Removal Cherokees, includes much valuable information in his *Reminiscences of the Indians* [313]. The Indian Territory attracted many short-term visitors, some of whom recorded impressions. Foreman has edited the journal of Ethan Allen Hitchcock [92], as well as John Howard Payne's *Indian Justice: A Cherokee Murder Trial at Tahlequah in 1840* [94]. David Knowles's account of a journey to the Cherokees in 1839–40 [184] contains some interesting observations, and George Foster's *Reminiscences of Travel in Cherokee Lands* offers vivid glimpses of Cherokee life in the 1880s [101].

The American Civil War brought into open conflict unresolved animosities stemming from the Treaty of New Echota and the bitterness of Removal. Unable to maintain neutrality, the Cherokee Nation officially joined the Confederacy, and the wealthier, mostly mixed-blood minority, or Treaty Party, became active in the Southern cause. The nonslaveholding, poorer majority of the Nation, including most of the full bloods, sympathized with the North, and many enlisted with the Union forces at first opportunity. Several desperate battles were fought in the Indian Territory and adjacent areas; at war's end the countryside was desolated. The primary reference work for this conflict and its aftermath is Abel's trilogy, *Slaveholding Indians* [2], which covers slavery, secession, participation in the Civil War, and Reconstruction. A sizable literature concerns Confederate Cherokees, some of which is summarized in articles by Morton [228] and Dale [58]. The celebrated Stand

Watie, the last Confederate general to surrender, is a central figure in Dale and Litton's *Cherokee Cavaliers* [59] and in Frank Cunningham's rebel-rousing *General Stand Watie's Confederate Indians* [56]. The situation of the Union sympathizers is less well documented, although Wiley Britton's *The Union Brigade in the Civil War* [26] contains good material. Paul Lambert reviews "The Cherokee Reconstruction Treaty of 1866" [192], and Hanna Warren [312] also deals with Reconstruction.

The turbulent post–Civil War decades were marked by legal fights over grazing lands, railroad building, increased lawlessness, and an influx of whites ("Boomers" or "Sooners") into the Cherokee Nation, such that the Cherokees had become an increasingly disfranchised minority in their own country by the early 1880s. These developments set the stage for passage of the Allotment Act and enabling legislation that dissolved the legal status of the Cherokee Nation and paved the way for eventual Oklahoma statehood. Wilcomb Washburn's *The Assault on Indian Tribalism: The General Allotment Law (Dawes Act) of 1887* [315] is the most concise background source; additional material on allotment can be found in D. S. Otis's *The Dawes Act and the Allotment of Indian Lands*, recently reissued and edited by Prucha [239], and in Debo's *And Still the Waters Run* [66]. Daniel Littlefield's informative essay "Utopian Dreams of the Cherokee Fullbloods, 1890–1934" [202] and Robert Thomas's brief description of the Redbird Smith Movement [293] trace some of the contours of full blood resistance to allotment and subsequent disaffection with the dominant Oklahoma society.

Cherokee adaptation in the early 1940s is described in a series of articles by geographer Leslie Hewes [139], [140], [141], [142], and Debo reports on socioeconomic conditions a decade later [67]. The demographic, economic, social, and political situation of the culturally conservative Cherokee population in the later 1960s is delineated and analyzed in a series of papers by Albert Wahrhaftig [301], [302], [303], [304], [305]. Wahrhaftig and Thomas [307] expose the myth of Cherokee assimilation into mainstream Oklahoma society, and Thomas has reviewed "The Role of the Church in Indian Adjustment" [294] and looked at modern Cherokee educational problems [295]. Murray Wax's *Indian Americans* [316] contains a chapter focusing on his research with the Oklahoma Cherokees, and a wealth of primary reports and testimony appears in the published *Hearings before the Special Senate Subcommittee on Indian Education* [134], headed by the late Senator Robert F. Kennedy. The message of these recent studies seems to be that, though the Oklahoma Cherokees suffer poverty and unequal opportunity, they maintain their Cherokee identity and share a distinctive and resilient set of values.

## The Eastern Cherokees

Left behind in the wake of the general Removal of 1838, a small group of Cherokees found refuge in the mountain fastness of western North Carolina. These people were for the most part conservative Cherokees. According to Mooney [225], these Cherokees were permitted to remain in their native land because of the martyrdom of Tsali, who reportedly surrendered himself for execution after killing some federal soldiers. This story may have been slightly romanticized by the time Mooney heard it from his informants. Nevertheless, the theme of Tsali's self-sacrifice is repeated in the accounts of Bass [18], Kutsche [190], and Bedford [20]. John P. Arthur [9] cites oral testimony suggesting a different interpretation of the Tsali episode. At any rate, this remaining group formed the nucleus of what later became legally recognized as the Eastern Band of the Cherokees, who continue to live today on the Qualla Boundary Reservation and in the Snowbird community of Graham County, North Carolina.

Mooney's historical sketch, with its rich blend of documentary evidence, oral history, and direct observation, is the definitive account of the Eastern Cherokees to 1900. Leonard Bloom presents a careful analysis of Eastern Cherokee acculturation in a lengthy article [23], and the same author isolates markers of cultural conservatism observed during his fieldwork in 1935 [24]. William Gilbert has come closest to providing a basic ethnography of the Eastern Cherokee [109]. He includes a fine synchronic description of Eastern Cherokee society as he encountered it in 1932, as well as a valuable reconstruction of eighteenth-century Cherokee society based mainly on information contained in the Payne-Butrick manuscripts in the Newberry Library. John Gulick's survey *Cherokees at the Crossroads* [121] offers a detailed empirical analysis of the Eastern Cherokees in the late 1950s; this volume has been reissued with an epilogue by Sharlotte Williams that updates some of the information and also summarizes some of her research in the Snowbird settlements. Considerable ethnographic and sociological material appears in Harriet Kupferer's medically oriented study "The 'Principal People' 1960" [187]. Kupferer has also written a brief general article on the Eastern Cherokees [188], and Oswalt offers a capsule treatment in his chapter on the Eastern Cherokees in the second edition of his textbook *This Land Was Theirs* [238]. Gilbert also has written an article-length retrospective account of the North Carolina Cherokees [110]. John P. Brown published an article in 1938 that presents thumbnail sketches of Eastern Cherokee chiefs [27].

The Eastern Cherokees remained fairly isolated throughout the nineteenth century, but a few visitors left some firsthand observations. Among the more valuable descriptions are those of Charles Lanman [194] and Ziegler and Grosscup [347]. Frederick Starr went to the Eastern Cherokees shortly before the turn of the century to do anthropometric measurements and published a short summary of his ethnographic notes [286]. Articles on the "Cherokee Indian School" by Fred Olds [237] afford a glimpse of Cherokee life in 1916, and Thelma Brown's *By Way of Cherokee* [29] contains some useful data.

William Holland Thomas, a white trader who had gained the confidence of the Cherokee, became their spokesman and nominal chief. He guided the destinies of the Eastern Cherokees after the Removal through the Civil War. Mattie Russell has published a short article on Thomas [266] that is based on fuller data contained in her doctoral dissertation. The Kilpatricks have translated and annotated official documents of the Wolftown community from 1850 to 1862 [173]; these documents afford a unique view of the inner workings of local government. Hiram Wilburn has published two articles [321], [325] containing historical material on the North Carolina Cherokees.

Several articles present geographic and demographic information on the Eastern Cherokees. Robert Lambert [193] surveys source material for a history of the Oconaluftee Valley from 1800 to 1860. In a short report for the eleventh census of 1890, Thomas Donaldson offers demographic and socioeconomic data [73]. Gaston Litton has reviewed "Enrollment Records for the Eastern Band of Cherokee Indians" [205], and Donald Ballas [12] has written on Eastern Cherokee subsistence.

Finally, the recent special Cherokee issue of the *Appalachian Journal* [251] offers some perspectives on contemporary Cherokee studies.

**Language**

Cherokee has long been recognized as a member of the Iroquoian family of languages. Floyd Lounsbury [207], utilizing linguistic dating techniques, demonstrates that Cherokee is the most divergent of the Iroquoian languages; he estimates that it split from the main line of Iroquoian languages approximately 3,500 to 3,800 years ago. Mary Haas [124] has written the best modern synthesis of language relationships in the Southeast, and James Crawford's introduction to *Studies in Southeastern Indian Languages* [53] presents a good overview, including a short discussion of Cherokee. In the same volume, Willard Walker [310] provides an excellent inventory of the status of Cherokee linguistic studies; Walker's article contains an extensive bibliography of publications on and in the Cherokee language. A much earlier list of sources appears in James C. Pilling's *Bibliography of Iroquoian Languages* [248]; unfortunately most of Pilling's sources are inaccessible. John Krueger [186] has made available two rare early grammars of Cherokee: the Pickering grammar of 1831 and one compiled by von der Gobelenz in 1852.

Two significant recent contributions to Cherokee linguistic studies deserve special mention: Durbin Feeling's *Cherokee-English Dictionary* [77] and *Beginning Cherokee* by Ruth Holmes and Betty Smith [146]. The Feeling volume not only is the best available dictionary but also contains a sophisticated outline of basic Cherokee grammar. Holmes and Smith have prepared a programmed sequence of lessons for learning Cherokee that includes good grammatical discussions and basic vocabulary. Jack Alexander [6] has compiled a dictionary in English and in the Sequoyan syllabary, which is based on the word lists of Mooney [225] and Brown [28] and supplemented with freshly collected lexical entries. Frank Speck [276] and Frans Olbrechts [236] have contributed short specimen Eastern Cherokee texts. Archibald Hill has exploded the academic myth about Cherokee's being a "primitive" language because of its complex conjugations [143].

Much research is now being done, and more will be done in the future on Cherokee sociolinguistics. Published sources relevant to this interest include Mooney's essay "Evolution of Cherokee Personal Names" [220], Gulick's "Language and Passive Resistance among the Eastern Cherokee" [120], "Verbs Are King at Panther Place" [171] by the Kilpatricks, and the brief article by the Kings, "Old Words for New Ideas: Linguistic Acculturation in Modern Cherokee" [180]. Jack Kilpatrick [160] has tried to resolve the etymology of the tribal name, Cherokee, along with other personal and place names.

The Cherokees are famous among American Indians for developing their own written language with the invention of a syllabary devised by the renowned Sequoyah in the 1820s. Many facts about Sequoyah's life are unknown, and his career lends itself to myth-making. George Foster wrote an early biography of Sequoyah [100]; Grand Foreman's *Sequoyah* [96] sums up most of what is known about this genius, but is not without some bias concerning Sequoyah's parentage; the Kilpatricks' *Sequoyah, of Earth and Intellect* [163] is written by two Cherokee scholars well versed in the intricacies of the syllabary. Traveller Bird's *Tell Them They Lie: The Sequoyah Myth* [296] is a polemical fabrication of a new myth whose meaning is discussed by Fogelson [86]. Holsoe [147] considers Sequoyah's invention as a case of stimulus diffusion.

The Sequoyan syllabary was eagerly embraced as a means of written communication by both Christian and non-Christian Cherokees. Spurred on by the efforts of the dedicated missionary Samuel A. Worcester [16], the pre-Removal Cherokee government established a printing press that published Cherokee laws, a newspaper (the

*Cherokee Phoenix*), translations of the Bible, and religious tracts. The Kilpatricks review Worcester's contributions in their *New Echota Letters* [176]. Robert Martin [210] discusses *The Cherokee Phoenix*, and Foster recounts the history of the Cherokee Bible [102]. An appreciation of the wide range of applications to which the syllabary was put by the Cherokees can be gained from the Kilpatricks' diverse collection of translated materials, *The Shadow of Sequoyah* [170]. John White briefly comments "On the Revival of Printing in the Cherokee Language" [318] in modern Oklahoma.

More technical aspects of the syllabary are discussed by Mooney in "Improved Cherokee Alphabets" [223] and by Wallace Chafe and Jack Kilpatrick's article "Inconsistencies in Cherokee Spelling" [36]. Modern educational applications of the Cherokee syllabary are mentioned in Walker's "Notes on Native Writing Systems and the Design of Native Literacy Programs" [309].

## Ecology, Natural History, and Material Culture

Gary Goodwin's recent *Cherokees in Transition* [115] is a useful synthesis of scattered data on aboriginal Cherokee ecology and the changes it underwent through 1775. The population, settlement, and ecology of modern Eastern Cherokees are discussed by Donald Ballas [11], and previously mentioned articles by Hewes [139], [140], [141], [142] consider Oklahoma Cherokee ecological adjustment in the early 1940s.

The floral and faunal resources of the Southern Appalachian region were extraordinarily rich and diverse. Over the centuries the Cherokees accumulated considerable knowledge about their environment. John Witthoft published an early Cherokee ethnobotanical note [338] from the diaries of the Gambolds, early Moravian missionaries. Mooney scatters a great deal of plant and animal lore throughout his "Myths of the Cherokee" [225]. Lydia Taylor's survey of the use of medicinal plants among the Southeastern tribes [292] leans heavily on Cherokee material. E. L. Core has published a short article on Cherokee ethnobotany [41]. Max White [319] has collected recent information on use of native food plants by the Eastern Cherokees, and Paul Hamel and Mary Chiltoskey have written a popular book entitled *Cherokee Plants and Their Uses* [127]. Mary Ulmer and Samuel Beck [298] have produced a Cherokee recipe book. Contributions to Cherokee ethnozoology include Pickens's article on Cherokee bird nomenclature [245], Witthoft's informative essay on Eastern Cherokee bird lore [335], and Speck's analysis of Cherokee ethno-herpetology [279].

No comprehensive summary of Cherokee material culture has ever been written. Gilbert's monograph [109] contains considerable information on material culture, plus a useful referencing of earlier sources that mention items of Cherokee material culture. *Sun Circles and Human Hands* by Emma Lila Fundaburk and Mary Douglas Fundaburk Foreman [106] presents pictorial and textual material from prehistoric and ethnographic horizons. Rodney Leftwich has published a useful popular guide to Cherokee arts and crafts [196], and Alanson Skinner briefly describes the Cherokee collection in the

American Museum of Natural History [273]. Cherokee basketry and decorative art are discussed by Speck [275], and the same author, with Leonard Broom, provides details on ceremonial paraphernalia in *Cherokee Dance and Drama* [281]. Pottery became a lost art among the Cherokees soon after the introduction of European metal utensils, but pottery was reintroduced to the Eastern Cherokees by the Catawbas in the 1840s, and this style continues to be made today for the tourist market. Catawba-Cherokee pottery manufacture is described in two articles by Mark Harrington [131], [132] and one by Vladimir Fewkes [81]. Speck [278] has written an interesting monograph on the varied uses of gourds in the Southeast, which relies heavily on Cherokee data, and Witthoft has published a far-ranging article, "Stone Pipes of the Historic Cherokee" [342]. Speck has also contributed an article on Cherokee blowguns [277], and Duane King [179] summarizes most of what is known about Cherokee bows.

**Social Organization**

Social organization is taken here in a wide sense to encompass house types, settlement pattern, marriage, kinship, descent groups, economic organization, legal system, and local level and tribal political systems.

Dickens [70] and De Baillou [64] contribute brief notes on traditional Cherokee architecture, while Lewis and Kneberg [199] have described the "hot house" or sweat lodge. Changes in settlement pattern in response to acculturation are outlined by Witthoft [343], and

Douglas Wilms reports on nineteenth-century Cherokee settlement pattern in Georgia [333].

Traditional Cherokee kinship, marriage, and descent groups are carefully analyzed in Gilbert's monograph on the Eastern Cherokees [109]. William Willis [332] has pointed to evidence of patrilineal inheritance among the eighteenth-century Cherokees who have otherwise been assumed to have been primarily matrilineal. Changes in kinship reckoning have been studied by Alexander Spoehr by using Gilbert's Eastern Cherokee data, documentary sources, and field data from Oklahoma [283]. Bloom briefly considers the effects of acculturation on the Cherokee clan system [22]. Articles by Speck and Shaeffer [282] and by Fogelson and Kutsche [90] present information on local town structure and economic organization.

Fred Gearing's *Priests and Warriors* [108] is a major work in the reconstruction of eighteenth-century Cherokee social structure and political organization. Not only does Gearing reveal the structure and functioning of Cherokee political life, he also analyzes the dynamic forces that transformed a loosely confederated set of autonomous villages into a centralized state. Fogelson [89] has discussed traditional Cherokee notions of power from the standpoint of religious ideology and politics, and Wahrhaftig and Lukens-Wahrhaftig [306] interpret Cherokee power and powerlessness in modern Oklahoma.

Two legally trained scholars have produced significant books on traditional Cherokee law. John Phillip Reid's *A Law of Blood: The Primitive Law of the Cherokee*

*Nation* [256] contains an impressive amount of documentary research; yet Reid too often forces his material into Western legal categories and tends to conceive of law as an institution separable from the rest of Cherokee society and culture. Some of these difficulties are less apparent in Rennard Strickland's *Fire and the Spirits: Cherokee Law from Clan to Court* [289]. Strickland is sensitive to the intimate connections between religion, ethics, and law in traditional Cherokee society. These two books complement one another and, taken together with Gearing [108], produce a balanced view of traditional Cherokee legal concepts and action.

**World View, Religion, and Medicine**

Despite the fact that a bewildering amount has been published about Cherokee spiritual beliefs and practice, no satisfactory general synthesis of Cherokee religion exists. Gilbert's monograph on the Eastern Cherokee [109] treats traditional religion, but like the Payne-Butrick manuscripts upon which he relies, his analysis is overschematized. Raw materials for a general account of Cherokee religion abound in Mooney's "Myths of the Cherokees" [225], and Speck and Broom's *Cherokee Dance and Drama* [281] provides an essential outline of the traditional Cherokee ceremonial cycle plus great detail on choreography. Cherokee ethos and world view receive some attention in Gulick's *Cherokees at the Crossroads* [121] and in Gearing's *Priests and Warriors* [108]. Hudson has insightfully discussed "The Cherokee Concept of Natural Balance" [151], and Meredith and Milam treat some fundamental beliefs in "A Cherokee Vision of Eloh" [216]. Fragmentary materials from Moravian sources are collated in De Baillou's "A Contribution to the Mythology and Conceptual World of the Cherokee Indians" [62].

Aspects of Cherokee magic and religious belief have received much discussion. Corkran has published two articles emphasizing the centrality of fire and sun in traditional Cherokee religion [43], [44], and the same author assesses "The Nature of the Cherokee Supreme Being" [45]. Mooney [224] discusses the significance of the river in Cherokee ritual, and Stansbury Hagar has written "Cherokee Star-lore" [123]. The beliefs in "little people" among both the Cherokee and the Iroquois are described by Witthoft and Hadlock [344]. Olbrechts [234] summarizes methods of Cherokee divination. Love magic of the Oklahoma Cherokees, based on magical texts or "formulas" written in the Sequoyan syllabary, receives monographic treatment by the Kilpatricks [172], and a companion volume by the same authors deals with a broader spectrum of Oklahoma Cherokee magic [175]. Fogelson [88] has tried to elucidate Cherokee sorcery and witchcraft beliefs and practices.

The Cherokees possess an extensive corpus of myths, folktales, and legends. Several major and minor collections have been published, as well as articles on single myths, and many secondary or derivative collections intended for a popular or children's market have also appeared. Mooney's magnificent "Myths of the Cherokees" [225] remains the basic collection. The best corresponding collection for the Oklahoma Cherokees is

*Friends of the Thunder* by Jack and Anna Kilpatrick [168]. An earlier set of Cherokee stories from Oklahoma was published by John B. Davis [60] and bears close thematic similarity to many of the myths recorded by Mooney. Walker has edited a recent collection of Cherokee stories related to him by an Oklahoma Cherokee minister, Walt Spade [274]; also from Oklahoma is the recent compilation of *Cherokee Spirit Tales* [118] gathered by Gregory and Strickland. Another important collection from the Eastern Cherokees is the set of folktales reconstructed from the field notes of Frans Olbrechts and edited by the Kilpatricks [174]. Corkran [42] and Witthoft [339] have independently discovered and commented upon fragments of Cherokee migration myths, and Witthoft has also presented a small collection of Eastern Cherokee bird stories [337]. James Hedges has recently analyzed "Attributive Mutation in Cherokee Natural History Myth" [135], and Ruth Suddeth has written a general article on Cherokee mythology [290].

Much more, however, remains to be done with Cherokee mythology and folklore. We still lack a suitable analysis of the contexts and performance features of Cherokee myth and storytelling (though there are some suggestive leads in Mooney). Also, the rich yield of Cherokee oral literature seems ripe for efforts to apply modern structural analysis.

Cherokee ritual and ceremonialism has received considerable study. James Howard [149] has attempted to link the general Southeastern ceremonial complex, particularly as it persists in Oklahoma, with late prehistoric iconography and symbolism; the Cherokees and Creeks figure prominently in his ambitious enterprise. Gertrude Kurath [189] has evaluated environmental effects on Cherokee-Iroquois ceremonialism. *Cherokee Dance and Drama*, as mentioned before, provides an excellent overview of ceremonialism as remembered and reenacted by Speck and Broom's Eastern Cherokee informants in the 1930s. Elsewhere [280], Speck has separately surveyed the ceremonial use of masks by the Eastern Cherokees, particularly those used in performances of the boisterous Booger Dance. Later information on Eastern Cherokee dances is available in an article by John Gillespie [111]. Cherokee adoption of the Calumet ritual, in the form of the Eagle Dance, is suggestively referred to in Witthoft's article on stone pipes [342], and Harriet Holman [145] reports reminiscences of the last full-scale Eagle Dance performed by the Eastern Band. Some details of Cherokee war ritual can be found in Nathaniel Knowles's general analysis, "The Torture of Captives by the Indians of Eastern North America" [185]. An activity closely akin to warfare was the ball game; Mooney has written an important article on Cherokee ball play [221], and more recent contributions to the subject are offered by Fogelson [85] and Herndon [138].

The major seasonal ceremony in the horticultural Southeast was the Green Corn Festival. The best comparative source is Witthoft's "Green Corn Ceremonialism in the Eastern Woodlands" [341]; Witthoft has also published a more focused description, "The Cherokee Green Corn Medicine and the Green Corn Festival"

[336]. Additional details on Green Corn ceremonies can be found in *Cherokee Dance and Drama* [281]. An important component in the Green Corn complex was the imbibing of the specially decocted "Black Drink" to induce vomiting. Hudson has explored the symbolic meaning of this practice in his recent article, "Vomiting for Purity: Ritual Emesis in the Aboriginal Southeastern United States" [152].

Oklahoma Cherokee ceremonialism has been greatly influenced by interaction with neighboring groups, particularly by the Creeks and remnant Natchez. Thomas [293] has written the best published account of the revival of Oklahoma Cherokee ceremonialism that occurred with the emergence of the Nighthawk or Redbird Smith Movement after the Allotment Act. McCoy and Fulling's account, *History of the Stomp Dance or Sacred Fire of the Cherokee Nation* [212], may also be consulted. Howard has reported on the revival of a Natchez-Cherokee ceremonial ground [150], and Janet Campbell and Archie Sam discuss the preservation of Cherokee ceremonialism at the same locale [33]. A major contribution to understanding Oklahoma Cherokee ceremonialism will occur when Charlotte Heth's extensive unpublished ethnomusicological research becomes available.

Medical beliefs and practices are another area of traditional Cherokee life that has shown remarkable persistence. One reason for this retention is the availability of the Sequoyan syllabary. Medicine men set down formular knowledge in notebooks, and much of this esoteric material was passed on to subsequent generations. James

Mooney was the first investigator to discover the significance of this valuable body of information, and he announced his findings to the scholarly world in "Sacred Formulas of the Cherokees" [222]. Olbrechts translated and published a collection of these texts that were originally obtained by Mooney from a venerable medicine man named Swimmer. This monograph, *The Swimmer Manuscript* [226], is notable not only for the carefully translated texts but also for Olbrechts's extensive commentary and his detailed introduction to the philosophy and practice of Cherokee medicine. Olbrechts published several short articles based on his fieldwork, including "Cherokee Belief and Practice with Regard to Childbirth" [235]. Fogelson has assessed some of the long-term patterns in "Change, Persistence, and Accommodation in Cherokee Medico-magical Beliefs" [84], and Kupferer [187] has studied the interaction of traditional and modern health care among the Eastern Cherokees.

The Kilpatricks pursued parallel investigations of traditional medicine among the Oklahoma Cherokees. A small collection of medical texts was translated and published by Jack Kilpatrick in 1962 [161], and a larger collection with valuable commentary, *Notebook of a Cherokee Shaman* [177], was later published in collaboration with his wife, Anna. They have also written a brief article "Cherokee Rituals Pertaining to Medicinal Roots" [166], and Jack Kilpatrick has examined "Christian Motifs in Cherokee Healing Rituals" [162]. "The Foundation of Life," an extremely sacred ritual performed at times of national crisis, has also been published by the Kilpatricks [167].

Much primary material on Cherokee medicine and magic written in the Sequoyan syllabary remains untranslated in archives and in the private possession of Cherokee families and medicine men. This material should prove important for future scholars with linguistic, medical, and religious interests.

**Personality and Biography**

Cherokee personality has attracted very little formal psychological study. Charles Holzinger [148] provides a psychodynamic interpretation of Cherokee personality based on field observation among the Eastern Cherokees; Kutsche [191] summarizes some of his findings about personality as revealed by extensive Rorschach testing of culturally conservative Eastern Cherokee males.

Few memorable Cherokee autobiographies exist, and biographical data range from short article-length sketches to book-length treatments of historical figures. Major biographical sources on Sequoyah, Chief Bowles, Tsali, the Ridges, and Stand Watie have already been discussed. Remaining selected biographical references will be mentioned in relative chronological order.

Biographical material for major eighteenth-century Cherokee figures is scant. Raymond Evans [76] has summarized virtually all that is known of Ostenaco, a famous war chief who visited England with Henry Timberlake. The renowned Beloved Woman, Nancy Ward, who was an influential spokesperson and befriended the whites, is the subject of an article by Ben McClary [211] and a popular book by Harold Felton [78]. Duane King and Danny Olinger [181] have written about Oconastota, a war chief who later became principal chief; they have located what seems to be his grave. However, such other prominent eighteenth-century Cherokees as Moytoy, Attacullaculla (or the Little Carpenter), Old Hop, Corn Tassel, Dragging Canoe, and John Watts have not received separate biographical treatment.

Rufus Anderson published the *Memoirs of Catherine Brown: A Christian Indian of the Cherokee Nation* in 1825 [8], shortly after the death of this early convert, and Althea Bass has written *A Cherokee Daughter of Mount Holyoke* [17]. Ample biographical information on Major Ridge, John Ridge, and Elias Boudinot can be found in Wilkins's *Cherokee Tragedy* [326] and in Dale and Litton's *Cherokee Cavaliers* [59], Ralph Gabriel [107] published an earlier book on the life of Boudinot, who was the first editor of the *Cherokee Phoenix* and a leading member of the Treaty Party. John Ross, whose tenure as chief spanned the eventful period from before the Removal through the beginning of the Civil War, is the subject of book-length biographies by Rachel Eaton [75] and Gertrude Ruskin [265]. A reassessment of Ross's career is suggested in a recent book by Gary Moulton [229]. *The Life and Times of Hon. William P. Ross*, a volume devoted to a man who held important political offices among the post–Civil War Western Cherokees, was edited by his wife [261]. The *Memoirs of Narcissa Owen, 1831–1907* [240] provides perspectives from an upper-class Cherokee woman. Littlefield and Underhill have recently published an informative article [203] on the tragic life of the full-blooded Cherokee outlaw Ned Christie. Litton has produced a series of brief sketches "Principal Chiefs of the Cherokee Nation" [204].

Post-Removal Eastern Cherokees have largely avoided the biographer's pen. Mooney includes some biographical material on leading nineteenth-century figures among the Eastern Cherokees in his "Myths of the Cherokee" [225]. Wilburn [322] has produced a short biography of Chief Junaluska, who served with Andrew Jackson at Horseshoe Bend and became a leader among the Cherokees who escaped Removal. This same man became the subject of a fictionalized biography, the first novel to bear a North Carolina imprint, by Senator Robert Strange in 1839 [287]. Witthoft [340] wrote a sensitive obituary of Will West Long, a gifted Cherokee informant who substantially aided the researches of Mooney, Olbrechts, Gilbert, Speck, and others.

Finally, McKenney and Hall's *Indian Tribes of North America* [213] includes capsule biographies and portraits of Sequoyah, Tahchee (or Dutch), Major Ridge, John Ridge, and Tooantuh (or Spring Frog).

## ALPHABETICAL LIST AND INDEX

*Denotes items suitable for secondary school students.

Item no.    Essay page no.

[1]  Abel, Annie Heloise. 1908. "The History of Events Resulting in Indian Consolidation West of the Mississippi." *Annual Report of the American Historical Association for the Year 1906* 1:233-450.    (20)

[2]  ———. 1915-25. *The Slaveholding Indians*. 3 vols. Cleveland: Arthur H. Clark Co.    (18, 23)

[3]  Adair, James. 1930. *Adair's History of the American Indians*, ed. Samuel Cole Williams. Johnson City, Tenn.: The Watauga Press. (Reprinted, New York: Johnson Reprint, 1969.)    (12)

[4]  Alden, John Richard. 1942. "The Eighteenth Century Cherokee Archives." *American Archivist* 5:240-244.    (5)

[5]  ———. 1944. *John Stuart and the Southern Colonial Frontier: A Study of Indian Relations, War, Trade, and Land Problems in the Southern Wilderness, 1754–1775*. (Ann Arbor: University of Michigan

Press. (Reprinted, New York: Gordian Press, 1966.) (14)

[6] Alexander, J. T. compiler. 1971. *A Dictionary of the Cherokee Indian Language*. Privately printed. (29)

[7] Alvord, Charles W. and Lee Bidgood. 1912. *The First Explorations of the Trans-Allegheny Region by the Virginians, 1650–1674*. Cleveland: The Arthur H. Clark Co. (11)

[8] Anderson, Rufus. 1825. *Memoir of Catherine Brown; A Christian Indian of the Cherokee Nation*. Boston: S. T. Armstrong, and Crocker and Brewster. (42)

[9] Arthur, John P. 1914. *Western North Carolina A History (from 1730–1913)*. Raleigh: Edwards-Broughton. (Reprinted, Spartansburg, S. C.: The Reprint Company, 1973.) (26)

[10] Ball, Donald B. 1976. *A Bibliography of Tennessee Anthropology, including Cherokee, Chickasaw, and Melungeon Studies. Tennessee Anthropological Association Miscellaneous Paper 1*. Knoxville; Tennessee Anthropological Association. (7)

[11] Ballas, Donald J. 1960. "Notes on the Population, Settlement, and Ecology of

the Eastern Cherokee Indians." *Journal of Geography* 59:238-67. (31)

[12] ———. 1962. "The Livelihood of the Eastern Cherokees." *Journal of Geography* 61:342-50. (28)

[13] Ballenger, Thomas L. 1946. *Around Tahlequah Council Fires*. Revised edition. Oklahoma City: Cherokee Publishing Co. (22)

[14] Bartram, William. 1853. "Observations on the Creek and Cherokee Indians." *American Ethnological Society Transactions* 3:1-81. (12)

[15] ———. 1958. *Travels*. ed. Francis Harper. New Haven: Yale University Press. (12)

[16] Bass, Althea. 1936. *Cherokee Messenger*. Norman: University of Oklahoma Press. (18, 30)

[17] ———. 1937. *A Cherokee Daughter of Mount Holyoke*. Muscatine, Iowa: The Prairie Press. (42)

[18] ———. 1942. "Tsali of the Cherokees." *Sewanee Review* 50: 5-14. (26)

[19] ———. 1954. "James Mooney in Oklahoma." *Chronicles of Oklahoma* 32: 246-62. (8)

[20]* Bedford, Denton R. 1972. *Tsali*. San Francisco: Indian Historian Press. (26)

[21] Berkhofer, Robert F. 1965. *Salvation and the Savage: An Analysis of Protestant Missions and American Indian Response, 1787–1862*. Lexington: University of Kentucky Press. (17)

[22] Bloom, Leonard. 1939. "The Cherokee Clan, A Study in Acculturation." *American Anthropologist* 41:266-68. (34)

[23] _____. 1942. "The Acculturation of the Eastern Cherokee: Historical Aspects." *North Carolina Historical Review* 19:323-58. (26)

[24] _____. 1945. "A Measure of Conservatism." *American Anthropologist* 47:630-35. (26)

[25] Blumenthal, Walter Hart. 1955. *American Indians Dispossessed: Fraud in Land Cessions Forced Upon the Tribes*. Philadelphia: George S. MacManus Co. (20)

[26] Britton, Wiley. 1922. *The Union Brigade in the Civil War*. Kansas City, Mo.: Franklin Hudson Publishing Co. (24)

[27] Brown, John P. 1938. "Eastern Cherokee Chiefs." *Chronicles of Oklahoma* 16:3-35. (27)

[28] _____. 1938. *Old Frontiers: The Story of the Cherokee Indians from Earliest Times to the Date of Their Removal to the West, 1838.* Kingsport, Tenn.: Southern Publishers, Inc. (Reprinted, New York: Arno Press, 1971.) (14, 29)

[29] Brown, Thelma S. 1944. *By Way of Cherokee*. Atlanta: Home Mission Board, Southern Baptist Convention. (27)

[30] Burke, Joseph C. 1969. "The Cherokee Cases: A Study in Law, Politics, and Morality." *Stanford Law Review* 21:500-31. (20)

[31] * Burt, Jesse, and Robert B. Ferguson. 1973. *Indians of the Southeast, Then and Now*. Nashville: Abingdon Press. (7)

[32] * _____. 1973. *The Removal of the Cherokee Indians from Georgia*. Nashville: Abingdon Press. (21)

[33] Campbell, Janet and Archie Sam. 1975–76. "The Primal Fire Lingers." *The Chronicles of Oklahoma* 53:463-75. (39)

Carrington, Henry B. 1892. "Eastern Band of Cherokees of North Carolina," in Thomas Donaldson, *Eastern Band of Cherokees of North Carolina*, pp. 11-24. U.S. Census Office, *Eleventh Census, Extra Census Bulletin*. Washington: U.S.

Government Printing Office. [Bound together with No. 73 listed below.] (28)

[34] Carselowey, James Manford. 1972. *Cherokee Old Timers*. Adair, Okla. Privately Printed. (22)

[35] * Carter, Samuel III. 1976. *Cherokee Sunset: A Nation Betrayed*. Garden City, N.Y.: Doubleday and Co. (21)

[36] Chafe, Wallace L. and Jack F. Kilpatrick. 1963. "Inconsistencies in Cherokee Spelling." In *Symposium on Language and Culture*, eds. Viola E. Garfield and Wallace L. Chafe. *Proceedings of 1962 Annual Meeting of the American Ethnological Society*, pp. 60-63. Seattle: University of Washington Press. (31)

[37] Clark, Thomas D., ed. 1956. *Travels in the Old South: A Bibliography*. 3 vols. Norman: University of Oklahoma Press. (8)

[38] * Clarke, Mary Whatley. 1971. *Chief Bowles and the Texas Cherokees*. Norman: University of Oklahoma Press. (22)

[39] Coe, Joffre L. 1961. "Cherokee Archeology." In *Symposium on Cherokee and Iroquois Culture*. eds. William N. Fenton and John Gulick. Smithsonian Institution, *Bureau of American Ethnology Bul-*

*letin* 180, pp. 51-60. Washington, D.C.: U.S. Government Printing Office. (7, 10)

[40] * Collier, Peter. 1973. *When Shall They Rest? The Cherokees' Long Struggle With America*. New York: Holt, Rinehart and Winston. (22)

[41] Core, Earl L. 1967. "Ethnobotany of the Southern Appalachian Aborigines." *Economic Botany* 21: 198-214. (32)

[42] Corkran, David H. 1952. "A Cherokee Migration Fragment." *Southern Indian Studies* 4:27-28. (37)

[43] _____. 1953. "The Sacred Fire of the Cherokee." *Southern Indian Studies* 5:21-26. (36)

[44] _____. 1955. "Cherokee Sun and Fire Observances." *Southern Indian Studies* 7:33-38. (36)

[45] _____. 1956. "The Nature of the Cherokee Supreme Being." *Southern Indian Studies* 8:27-35. (36)

[46] _____. 1957. "Cherokee Pre-History." *North Carolina Historical Review* 34:455-66. (11)

[47] _____. 1962. *The Cherokee Frontier: Conflict and Survival, 1740–62*. Norman: University of Oklahoma Press. (5, 14)

[48] _____., ed. 1969. "Alexander Longe's 'A Small Postscript on the Ways and Manners of the Indians called Cherokees, the contents of the whole so that you may find everything by the pages.'" *Southern Indian Studies* 21:1-49. (13)

[49] _____. 1970. *The Carolina Indian Frontier*. Tricentennial Booklet No. 6. Columbia, S.C.: University of South Carolina Press. (14)

[50] Corn, James Franklin. 1953. "Removal of the Cherokees from the East." *The Filson Club History Quarterly* 27:36-51. (21)

[51] Cotterill, Robert S. 1954. *The Southern Indians: The Story of the Civilized Tribes Before Removal*. Norman: University of Oklahoma Press. (5)

[52] Crane, Verner W. 1928. *The Southern Frontier: 1670–1732*. Durham: Duke University Press. (Reprinted, Ann Arbor: University of Michigan Press, 1956.) (11)

[53] Crawford, James M. 1975. "Southeastern Indian Languages." In *Studies in Southeastern Languages*, ed. James M. Crawford, pp. 1-120. Athens: University of Georgia Press. (28)

[54] Cumming, William P. 1958. *The Southeast in Early Maps, with an Annotated Check List*

*of Printed and Manuscript Regional and Local Maps of Southeastern North America during the Colonial Period.* Princeton: Princeton University Press. (15)

[55] _____. 1966. "Mapping of the Southeast: The First Two Centuries." *The Southeastern Geographer* 6:3-19. (15)

[56] * Cunningham, Frank H. 1959. *General Stand Watie's Confederate Indians.* San Antonio: Naylor Co. (24)

[57] Cunningham, Hugh T. 1930. A History of the Cherokee Indians." *Chronicles of Oklahoma* 8:291-314; 407-440. (22)

[58] Dale, Edward Everett. 1947. "The Cherokees in the Confederacy." *Journal of Southern History* 13:159-185. (23)

[59] Dale, Edward Everett, and Gaston Litton. 1940. *Cherokee Cavaliers: Forty Years of Cherokee History as Told in the Correspondence of the Ridge-Watie-Boudinot Family.* Norman: University of Oklahoma Press. (24, 42)

[60] * Davis, John B. 1910. "Some Cherokee Stories." *Annals of Archaeology and Anthropology of the University of Liverpool* 3:26-49. (37)

[61] De Baillou, Clemens. 1955. "The Ex-

cavations at New Echota in 1954." *Early Georgia* 1(4):18-29. (10)

[62] _____. 1961. "A Contribution to the Mythology and Conceptual World of the Cherokee Indians." *Ethnohistory* 8:92-102. (36)

[63] _____, ed. 1961. *John Howard Payne to His Countrymen*. Athens: University of Georgia Press. (21)

[64] _____. 1967. "Notes on Cherokee Architecture." *Southern Indian Studies* 19:25-33. (33)

[65] _____. 1970. "The Dairies of the Moravian Brotherhood at the Cherokee Mission in Spring Place, Georgia for the Years 1800–1804." *Georgia Historical Quarterly* 54:571-76. (18)

[66] * Debo, Angie. 1940. *And Still the Waters Run*. Princeton: Princeton University Press. (22, 24)

[67] _____. 1951. *The Five Civilized Tribes of Oklahoma: Report on Social and Economic Conditions*. Philadelphia: Indian Rights Association. (25)

[68] De Brahm, Gerard William. 1971. *Report of the General Survey in the Southern District of North America*, ed. Louis De Vorsey, Jr.

Columbia, S.C.: University of South Carolina Press. (12)

[69] _____. 1966. *The Indian Boundary in the Southern Colonies, 1763–1775.* Chapel Hill: University of North Carolina Press. (15)

[70] Dickens, Jr., Roy S. 1967. "A Note on Cherokee House Construction of 1776." *Southern Indian Studies* 19:35. (33)

[71] Dickens, Jr., Roy S. 1976. *Cherokee Prehistory: The Pisgah Phase in the Appalachian Summit Region.* Knoxville: University of Tennessee Press. (10)

[72] Dockstader, Frederick J. and Alice W., compilers, 1973-1974. *The American Indian in Graduate Studies*, 2nd ed. 2 vols. *Contributions from the Museum of the American Indian, Heye Foundation* 25. New York: Museum of the American Indian, Heye Foundation. (6)

[73] Donaldson, Thomas. 1892. "Statistics of Indians," in Thomas Donaldson, *Eastern Band of Cherokees of North Carolina*, pp. 7-9, U.S. Census Office, *Eleventh Census, Extra Census Bulletin*. Washington: U.S. Government Printing Office. [Bound together with Carrington, Henry B., listed above.] (28)

[74] Downes, Rudolph C. 1936. "Cherokee-

American Relations in the Upper Tennessee Valley, 1776-1791." *East Tennessee Historical Society's Publications* 8:35-53. (16)

[75] * Eaton, Rachel Caroline. 1914. *John Ross and the Cherokee Indians.* Menasha, Wisc.: George Banta Publishing Co. (42)

[76]   Evans, E. Raymond. 1976. "Notable Persons in Cherokee History: Ostenaco." *Journal of Cherokee Studies* 1:41-54. (41)

[77]   Feeling, Durbin. 1975. *Cherokee-English Dictionary*, ed. William Pulte. Tahlequah, Okla.: Cherokee Nation of Oklahoma. (29)

[78]   Felton, Harold W. 1975. *Nancy Ward, Cherokee.* New York: Dodd, Mead and Co. (42)

[79]   Fenton, William N., L. H. Butterfield, and Wilcomb E. Washburn. 1957. *American Indian and White Relations to 1830: Needs and Opportunities for Study.* Chapel Hill: University of North Carolina Press. (8)

[80]   Fenton, William N. and John Gulick, eds. 1961. *Symposium on Cherokee and Iroquois Culture*, Smithsonian Institution, *Bureau of American Ethnology Bulletin 180.* Washington, D. C.: U.S. Government Printing Office. See items no. [39], [84], [90], [148], [189], [207], [293], [343].

[81]   Fewkes, Vladimir J. 1944. "Catawba Pot-

tery-Making, with Notes on Pamunkey Pottery-Making, Cherokee Pottery-Making, and Coiling." *Proceedings of the American Philosophical Society* 88:69-124. (33)

[82] * Filler, Louis and Allen Guttmann, eds. 1962. *The Removal of the Cherokee Nation: Manifest Destiny or National Dishonor?* Boston: D.C. Heath and Co. (20)

[83] * Fleischmann, Glen. 1971. *The Cherokee Removal, 1838: An Entire Indian Nation is Forced Out of Its Homeland.* New York: Watts. (21)

[84] Fogelson, Raymond D. 1961. "Change, Persistence, and Accommodation in Cherokee Medico-Magical Beliefs." In *Symposium on Cherokee and Iroquois Culture*, eds. William N. Fenton and John Gulick. Smithsonian Institution, *Bureau of American Ethnology Bulletin 180*, pp. 213-25. Washington, D.C.: U.S. Government Printing Office. (40)

[85] _____. 1971. "The Cherokee Ballgame Cycle: An Ethnologist's View." *Ethnomusicology* 15:327-38. (38)

[86] _____. 1974. "On the Varieties of Indian History: Sequoyah and Traveller Bird." *Journal of Ethnic Studies* 2:105-12. (30)

[87] * _____. 1975. "Southeast American Indians." *The New Encyclopaedia Britannica*, 15th ed., Vol. 17, pp. 218-22. ( 7)

[88] _____. 1975. "An Analysis of Cherokee Sorcery and Witchcraft." In *Four Centuries of Southern Indians*, ed. Charles M. Hudson, pp. 113-31. Athens: University of Georgia Press. (36)

[89] _____. 1977. "Cherokee Notions of Power." In *The Anthropology of Power*, eds. Raymond D. Fogelson and Richard N. Adams, pp. 185-194. New York: Academic Press. (34)

[90] Fogelson, Raymond D. and Paul Kutsche. 1961. "Cherokee Economic Cooperation: The Gadugi." In *Symposium on Cherokee and Iroquois Culture*, eds. William N. Fenton and John Gulick, Smithsonian Institution, *Bureau of American Ethnology Bulletin 180*, pp. 83-123. Washington, D.C.: U.S. Government Printing Office. (34)

[91] Foreman, Carolyn T. 1943. *Indians Abroad, 1493–1938*. Norman: University of Oklahoma Press. (13)

[92] Foreman, Grant, ed. 1930. *A Traveler in the Indian Territory: The Journal of Ethan*

*Allen Hitchcock, Late Major-General in the United States Army.* Cedar Rapids: The Torch Press. (23)

[93] ———. 1933. *Advancing the Frontier.* Norman: University of Oklahoma Press. (22)

[94] * ———, ed. 1934. *Indian Justice: A Cherokee Murder Trial at Tahlequah in 1840, as reported by John Howard Payne.* Oklahoma City: Harlow. (23)

[95] ———. 1936. *Indians and Pioneers: The Story of the American Southeast before 1830.* Revised ed. Norman: University of Oklahoma Press. (21)

[96] * ———. 1938. *Sequoyah.* Norman: University of Oklahoma Press. (30)

[97] ———. 1946. *The Last Trek of the Indians.* Chicago: University of Chicago Press. (Reprinted, New York: Russell and Russell, 1972.) (21)

[98] ———. 1953. *The Five Civilized Tribes.* Revised ed. Norman: University of Oklahoma Press. (22)

[99] ———. 1953. *Indian Removal: The Emigration of the Five Civilized Tribes of Indians.* New Edition. Norman: University of Oklahoma Press. (20)

[100] Foster, George Everett. 1885. *Se-Quo-Yah, the American Cadmus and Modern Moses. A Complete Biography of the Greatest of Redmen, Around Whose Wonderful Life Has Been Woven the Manners, Customs, and Beliefs of the Early Cherokees, Together With a Recital of Their Wrongs and Wonderful Progress Toward Civilization.* Philadelphia: Indian Rights Association. (30)

[101] ———. 1899. *Reminiscences of Travel in Cherokee Lands. An Address Delivered Before the Ladies' Missionary Society of the Ithaca, N.Y., Congregational Church, 1898.* Ithaca, N.Y.: Democrat Press. (23)

[102] ———. 1899. *Story of the Cherokee Bible. An Address, with Additional Explanatory Notes, Delivered Before the Meeting of the Ladies' Missionary Society of the First Congregational Church, Ithaca, N.Y., Feb. 5, 1897.* 2nd ed. Ithaca, N.Y.: Democrat Press. (31)

[103] Franklin W. Neil. 1932. "Virginia and the Cherokee Indian Trade, 1673-1752." *East Tennessee Historical Society's Publications* 4:3-21. (12)

[104] ———. 1933. "Virginia and the Cherokee Indian Trade, 1753-1775." *East*

*Tennessee Historical Society's Publications* 5:22-38.

[105] Franks, Kenny A. 1974. "Political Intrigue in the Cherokee Nation, 1839." *Journal of the West* 12(4):17-25. (22)

[106] * Fundaburk, Emma Lila and Mary Douglas Fundaburk Foreman, eds. 1957. *Sun Circles and Human Hands: The Southeastern Indians Art and Industries.* Luverne, Ala.: Emma Lila Fundaburk. (32)

[107] * Gabriel, Ralph H. 1941. *Elias Boudinot, Cherokee and His America.* Norman: University of Oklahoma Press. (42)

[108] Gearing, Frederick O. 1962. *Priests and Warriors: Social Structures for Cherokee Politics in the 18th Century. American Anthropological Association Memoir 93.* Menasha, Wisc.: American Anthropological Association. (34, 35)

[109] Gilbert, William H., Jr. 1943. *The Eastern Cherokees.* Smithsonian Institution, *Bureau of American Ethnology Bulletin* 133, Paper 23, pp. 169-413. Washington, D.C.: U.S. Government Printing Office. (26, 32)

[110] * _____. 1957. "The Cherokees of North Carolina: Living Memorials of the Past." In *Smithsonian Report for 1956,*

pp. 529-55. Washington, D.C.: U.S. Government Printing Office. (27)

[111] Gillespie, John D. 1961. "Some Eastern Cherokee Dances Today." *Southern Indian Studies* 13:29-43. (38)

[112] Gilmer, George Rockingham. 1855. *Sketches of Some of the First Settlers of Upper Georgia, of the Cherokees, and the Author.* New York: D. Appleton and Co. (Revised and corrected edition, Americus, Ga.: Americus Book Co., 1926.) (16)

[113] Gleeson, Paul, ed. 1970. *Archaeological Investigations in the Tellico Reservoir, Interim Report, 1969. Report of Investigations* 8. Knoxville: Department of Anthropology, University of Tennessee. (10)

[114] _____, ed. 1971. *Archaeological Investigations in the Tellico Reservoir, Interim Report, 1970. Report of Investigations* 9. Knoxville: Department of Anthropology, University of Tennessee. (10)

[115] Goodwin, Gary C. 1977. *Cherokees in Transition: A Study of Changing Culture and Environment Prior to 1775. Research Paper* 181. University of Chicago, Department of Geography. (31)

[116] Grant, Ludovick. 1909. "Historical Relation of Facts Delivered by Ludovick Grant, Indian Trader, to His Excellency, the Governor of South Carolina." *South Carolina Historical and Genealogical Magazine* 10:54-68. (13)

[117] * Gregory, Jack and Rennard Strickland. 1967. *Sam Houston with the Cherokees, 1824-1833*. Austin: University of Texas Press. (22)

[118] * _____. 1969. *Cherokee Spirit Tales: Tribal Myths, Legends, and Folklore*. Fayetteville, Ark.: Indian Heritage Association. (37)

[119] Grindle, Donald, Jr., 1975. "Cherokee Removal and American Politics." *The Indian Historian* 8(3):33-42;56. (20)

[120] Gulick, John. 1958. "Language and Passive Resistance among the Eastern Cherokees." *Ethnohistory* 5:60-81. (30)

[121] _____. 1960. *Cherokees at the Crossroads*. Chapel Hill: Institute for Research in Social Science, University of North Carolina. (Reprinted, with an Epilogue by Sharlotte Neely Williams, 1973.) (26, 35)

[122] Guthe, Alfred K., and Patricia B. Kelly. 1963. *An Anthropological Bibliography of the Eastern Seaboard, Vol. 2. Eastern States*

*Archaeological Federation Research Publication* No. 2. Trenton: Eastern States Archaeological Federation. ( 7)

[123] Hagar, Stansbury. 1906. "Cherokee Star-lore." In *Boas Anniversary Volume; Anthropological Papers Written in Honor of Franz Boas*, ed. Berthold Laufer, pp. 354-66. New York: Stechert. (36)

[124] Haas, Mary R. 1973. "The Southeast." In *Current Trends in Linguistics*, Vol. 10. *Linguistics in North America*, Part 2, ed. Thomas A. Sebeok, pp. 1210-49. The Hague: Mouton. (28)

[125] Halliburton, R., Jr., 1976. *Red Over Black: Black Slavery Among the Cherokee Indians*. Westport, Conn.: Greenwood Press. (19)

[126] Hally, David J. 1971. "The Archaeology of European-Indian Contact in the Southeast." In *Red, White, and Black: Symposium on Indians in the Old South*, ed. Charles H. Hudson, *Southern Anthropological Society Proceedings* No. 5, pp. 55-66. Athens: University of Georgia Press. (10)

[127] * Hamel, Paul B. and Chiltoskey, Mary U. 1975. *Cherokee Plants and Their Uses: A 400 Year History*. Sylva, N.C.: Herald Publishing Co. (32)

[128] Hamer, P. M. 1925. "Anglo-French Rivalry in the Cherokee Country, 1754-1757." *North Carolina Historical Review* 2:303-22. (14)

[129] _____. 1925. "Fort Loudoun in the Cherokee War, 1758-1761." *North Carolina Historical Review* 2:442-58. (14)

[130] Hargrett, Lester, compiler. 1972. *The Gilcrease-Hargrett Catalogue of Imprints*. Norman: University of Oklahoma Press. ( 5)

[131] Harrington, Mark Raymond. 1908. "Catawba Potters and Their Work." *American Anthropologist* 10:399-407. (33)

[132] _____. 1909. "The Last of the Iroquois Potters." Education Department Bulletin, Museum Bulletin 133, University of the State of New York. *New York State Museum, Annual Report, 1908,* 61(1):222-27. (33)

[133] Haywood, John. 1959. *Natural and Aboriginal History of Tennessee, up to the First Settlements Therein by the White People in the Year 1768. Including Archaeological, Geological and Historical Annotations Bringing the Ancient Account into Focus with Present Day Knowledge, and an Introductory Sketch of the Author, John*

*Haywood*, ed. Mary U. Rothrock. Jackson, Tenn.: McCowat-Mercer Press. (Reprinted, Kingsport, Tenn.: F. M. Hill-Books, 1973.) (15)

[134] 1969. *Hearings before the Special Subcommittee on Indian Education on the Committee on Labor and Public Welfare, United States Senate, Ninetieth Congress. First and Second Sessions on the Study of the Education of Indian Children*. Part 2. February 19, 1968, Twin Oaks, Calif. Washington, D.C.: U.S. Government Printing Office. (25)

[135] Hedges, James S. 1973. "Attributive Mutation in Cherokee Natural History Myth." *North Carolina Folklore Journal* 21:147-54. (37)

[136] * Henderson, Archibald. 1920. *The Conquest of the Old Southwest: the Romantic Story of the Early Pioneers into Virginia, the Carolinas, Tennessee, and Kentucky, 1740-1790*. (14)

[137] Henderson, Archibald. 1931. "The Treaty of Long Island of Holston, July 1777." *North Carolina Historical Review* 8:55-116. (16)

[138] Herndon, Marcia. 1971. "The Cherokee Ballgame Cycle: An Eth-

nomusicologist's View." *Ethnomusicology* 15:339-52. (38)

[139] Hewes, Leslie. 1942. "Indian Land in the Cherokee Country of Oklahoma." *Economic Geography* 18:401-12. (25, 31)

[140] _____. 1942. "The Oklahoma Ozarks as the Land of the Cherokees." *Geographical Review* 32:269-81. (25, 31)

[141] _____. 1943. "Cultural Fault Line in the Cherokee Country." *Economic Geography* 19:136-42. (25, 31)

[142] _____. 1944. "Cherokee Occupance in the Oklahoma Ozarks and Prairie Plains." *Chronicles of Oklahoma* 22:324-37. (25, 31)

[143] Hill, Archibald A. 1952. "A Note on Primitive Languages." *International Journal of American Linguistics* 18:172-77. (29)

[144] Holm, Tom. 1976. "Cherokee Colonization in Oklahoma." In *America's Exiles: Indian Colonization in Oklahoma*, ed. Arrell M. Gibson, pp. 60-76. Oklahoma City: Oklahoma Historical Society. (22)

[145] Holman, Harriet R. 1976. "Cherokee Dancing Remembered: Why the East-

ern Band Abjured the Old Eagle Dance." *North Carolina Folklore Journal* 26:101-06. (38)

[146] Holmes, Ruth B. and Betty S. Smith. 1976. *Beginning Cherokee*. Norman: University of Oklahoma Press. (29)

[147] Holsoe, Svend E. 1971. "A Case of Stimulus Diffusion (A Note on Possible Connections Between the Vai and Cherokee Scripts)." *Indian Historian* 4(3):56-57. (30)

[148] Holzinger, Charles H. 1961. "Some Observations on the Persistence of Aboriginal Cherokee Personality Traits." In *Symposium on Cherokee and Iroquois Culture*, eds. William N. Fenton and John Gulick. Smithsonian Institution, *Bureau of American Ethnology Bulletin* 180, pp. 227-37. Washington, D.C.: U.S. Government Printing Office. (41)

[149] Howard, James H. 1968. *The Southeastern Ceremonial Complex and Its Interpretation*. *Missouri Archaeological Society Memoir*: 6. Columbia, Mo.: Missouri Archaeological Society. (37)

[150] ———. 1970. "Bringing Back the Fire: The Revival of a Natchez-Cherokee Ceremonial Ground." *American Indian Crafts and Culture* 4:9-12. (39)

[151]   Hudson, Charles. 1970. "Cherokee Concept of Natural Balance." *The Indian Historian* 3(4):51-54.   (35)

[152]   _____. 1975. "Vomiting for Purity: Ritual Emesis in the Aboriginal Southeastern United States." In *Symbols and Society*, ed. Carole E. Hill. *Southern Anthropological Society Proceedings* No. 9, pp. 93-102. Athens: University of Georgia Press.   (39)

[153] * _____. 1977. *The Southeastern Indians*. Knoxville: University of Tennessee Press.   (7)

[154]   Jacobs, Wilbur R., ed. 1967. *The Appalachian Indian Frontier, The Edmond Atkin Report and Plan of 1755*. Lincoln: University of Nebraska Press.   (14)

[155] * Jahoda, Gloria. 1975. *The Trail of Tears*. New York: Holt, Rinehart and Winston.   (21)

[156]   Jones, William K. 1967. "General Guide to Documents on the Five Civilized Tribes in the University of Oklahoma Library, Division of Manuscripts." *Ethnohistory* 14:47-76.   ( 5)

[157]   Keel, Bennie C. 1976. *Cherokee Archaeology: A Study of the Appalachian*

*Summit*. Knoxville: University of Tennessee Press. (10)

[158] Kelly, A. R. and Clemens De Baillou. 1960. "Excavation of the Presumptive Site of Estatoe." *Southern Indian Studies* 12:3-30. (10)

[159] Kelly, Arthur R. and Robert S. Neitzel. 1961. *Chauga Mound and Village Site in Oconee County, South Carolina. University of Georgia Laboratory of Archaeology Series*, Report 3. Athens: University of Georgia. (10)

[160] Kilpatrick, Jack F. 1962. "An Ethnological Note on the Tribal Name of the Cherokees and Certain Place and Proper Names Derived from Cherokee." *Journal of the Graduate Research Center* 30:37-41. (30)

[161] _____. 1962. "The Siquanid Dil 'tidegi Collection." *Sacred Formulas of the Western Cherokees* Series 1, Number 1. Dallas: Southern Methodist University, Bridwell Library. (40)

[162] _____. 1965. "Christian Motifs in Cherokee Healing Rituals." *Perkins School of Theology, Journal* 18(2):32-36. (40)

[163] * Kilpatrick, Jack F. 1965. *Sequoyah, of Earth and Intellect*. Austin: Encino Press. (30)

[164] ——. ed. 1966. *The Wahnenauhi Manuscript: Historical Sketches of the Cherokees, Together with Some of Their Customs, Traditions, and Superstitions.* Smithsonian Institution, Bureau of American Ethnology, Bulletin 196, Paper 77, pp. 175-214. Washington, D.C.: U.S. Government Printing Office. (23)

[165] ——. 1967. "An Adventure Story of the Arkansas Cherokees, 1829." *Arkansas Historical Quarterly* 26: 40-47. (21)

[166] Kilpatrick, Jack F. and Anna G. 1964. "Cherokee Rituals Pertaining to Medicinal Roots." *Southern Indian Studies* 16:24-28. (40)

[167] ——. 1964. "The Foundation of Life:' The Cherokee National Ritual." *American Anthropologist* 66:1386-91. (40)

[168] * ——. 1964. *Friends of the Thunder: Folktales of Oklahoma Cherokee.* Dallas: Southern Methodist University Press. (37)

[169] ——, eds. 1965. "Letters from an Arkansas Cherokee Chief (1828-1829)." *Great Plains Journal* 5:26-24. (21)

[170] ——, eds. 1965. *The Shadow of Sequoyah: Social Documents of the Cherokees, 1862-1964.* Norman: University of Oklahoma Press. (31)

[171] ———. 1965. "Verbs are King at Panther Place: The Cherokee Tongue versus 'English' ". *Southwest Review* 50:372-76. (30)

[172] ———. 1965. *Walk in Your Soul: Love Incantations of the Oklahoma Cherokees.* Dallas: Southern Methodist University Press. (36)

[173] ———. 1966. *Chronicles of Wolftown: Social Documents of the North Carolina Cherokees, 1850-1862.* Smithsonian Institution, *Bureau of American Ethnology Bulletin* 196, Paper 75, pp. 1-111. Washington, D.C.: U.S. Government Printing Office. (28)

[174] ———. 1966. *Eastern Cherokee Folktales: Reconstructed from the Field Notes of Frans M. Olbrechts.* Smithsonian Institution, *Bureau of American Ethnology Bulletin* 196, Paper 80, pp. 379-447. Washington, D.C.: U.S. Government Printing Office. (37)

[175] ———. 1967. *Run Toward the Nightland: Magic of the Oklahoma Cherokees.* Dallas: Southern Methodist University Press. (36)

[176] ———, eds. 1968. *New Echota Letters,* Contributions of Samuel A. Worcester to the *Cherokee Phoenix.* Dallas: Southern Methodist University Press. (31)

[177] ———. 1970. *Notebook of a Cherokee Shaman*. Smithsonian Institution, *Contributions to Anthropology* 2, pp. 83-125. Washington, D.C.: Smithsonian Institution Press. (40)

[178] King, Duane H. 1976. "Cherokees and the Frontier of 1776." *Unto These Hills: A Drama of the Cherokee Nation, Bicentennial Edition*. Henderson, N.C.: Cherokee Historical Association. (16)

[179] ———. 1976. "Cherokee Bows." *Journal of Cherokee Studies* 1:92-97. (33)

[180] King, Duane H. and Laura H. 1976. "Old Words for New Ideas: Linguistic Acculturation in Modern Cherokee." *Tennessee Anthropologist* 1:58-62. (30)

[181] King, Duane H. and Danny E. Olinger. 1972. "Oconastota." *American Antiquity* 37:222-28. (42)

[182] Klinck, Carl F. and James J. Talman, eds. 1970. *The Journal of Major John Norton, 1816. Publications of the Champlain Society* 46. Toronto: The Champlain Society. (19)

[183] Knight, Oliver. 1954-55. "Cherokee Society Under the Stress of Removal, 1820-1846." *Chronicles of Oklahoma* 32:414-28. (21)

[184]   Knowles, David E. 1915-16. "Some Account of a Journey to the Cherokees, 1839-40; Being Extracts from the Journal of David E. Knowles." *Bulletin of Friends' Historical Society of Philadelphia* 6:70-78; 7:15-21, 42-50.   (23)

[185]   Knowles, Nathaniel. 1940. "The Torture of Captives by the Indians of Eastern North America." *Proceedings of the American Philosophical Society* 82:151-225.   (38)

[186]   Krueger, John R. 1963. "Two Early Grammars of Cherokee." *Anthropological Linguistics* 5:1-57.   (29)

[187]   Kupferer, Harriet J. 1966. *The "Principal People," 1960: a Study of Cultural and Social Groups of the Eastern Cherokee*. Smithsonian Institution, *Bureau of American Ethnology Bulletin* 196, Papers 78, pp. 215-325. Washington, D.C.: U.S. Government Printing Office.   (27, 40)

[188] *   _____. 1968. The Isolated Eastern Cherokee." In *The American Indian Today*, eds. Stuart Levine and Nancy Oestreich Lurie, pp. 87-97. Deland, Fla.: Everett/Edwards.   (27)

[189]   Kurath, Gertrude P. 1961. "Effects of Environment on Cherokee-Iroquois

Ceremonialism, Music and Dance." In *Symposium on Cherokee and Iroquois Culture*, eds. William N. Fenton and John Gulick. Smithsonian Institution, *Bureau of American Ethnology Bulletin* 180, pp. 173-95. Washington, D.C.: U.S. Government Printing Office. (38)

[190] Kutsche, Paul. 1963. "The Tsali Legend: Culture Heroes and Historiography." *Ethnohistory* 10:329-57. (26)

[191] _____. 1964. "Southern Appalachian Personality." *35th International Congress of Americanists, Mexico, D.F. Actas y Memorias* 2:103-09. (41)

[192] Lambert, Paul F. 1973. "The Cherokee Reconstruction Treaty of 1866." *Journal of the West* 12:471-89. (24)

[193] Lambert, Robert S. 1958. "The Oconaluftee Valley, 1800-1860: A Study of the Sources for Mountain History." *North Carolina Historical Review* 35: 415-26. (28)

[194] Lanman, Charles. 1849. *Letters from the Alleghany Mountains*. New York: G. P. Putnam. (Reprinted in Lanman, *Adventures in the Wilds of the United States and British American Provinces*, 1856, v. 1, pp. 343-473). (27)

[195] Lawr, V. Salo, ed. 1969. *Archaeological Investigations in the Tellico Reservoir, Tennessee, 1967-1968: An Interim Report.* Knoxville: Department of Anthropology, University of Tennessee. (10)

[196] * Leftwich, Rodney L. 1970. *Arts and Crafts of the Cherokee.* Cullowhee, N.C.: Land-of-the-Sky Press. (32)

[197] Lewis, Thomas M. N. 1960. "Editor's Notes: Settico Site on Little Tennessee River." *Tennessee Archaeologist* 16:92-103. (10)

[198] Lewis, Thomas M. N. and Madeleine Kneberg. 1946. *Hiawassee Island: an Archaelogical Account of Four Tennessee Indian Peoples.* Knoxville: University of Tennessee Press. (10)

[199] _____. 1953. "The Cherokee 'Hothouse'." *Tennessee Archaeologist* 9:2-5. (33)

[200] _____. 1958. *Tribes That Slumber: Indian Times in the Tennessee Region.* Knoxville: University of Tennessee Press. ( 9)

[201] Lillybridge, C. 1931. "Journey of a Party of Cherokee Emigrants", ed. by Grant Foreman. *Mississippi Valley Historical Review* 18:232-45. (21)

[202]   Littlefield, Daniel F. 1971. "Utopian Dreams of the Cherokee Fullbloods: 1890-1934." *Journal of the West* 10:404-427.   (24)

[203]   Littlefield, Jr., Daniel F. and Lonnie E. Underhill. 1974. "Ned Christie and His One-Man Fight with the United States Marshals." *Journal of Ethnic Studies* 1:2-13.   (43)

[204]   Litton, Gaston L. 1937. "The Principal Chiefs of the Cherokee Nation." *Chronicles of Oklahoma* 15:253-70.   (43)

[205]   _____. 1940. "Enrollment Records of the Eastern Band of Cherokee Indians." *North Carolina Historical Review* 17:199-231.   (28)

[206]   Logan, John H. 1859. *A History of the Upper Country of South Carolina, from the Earliest Periods to the Close of the War of Independence.* Vol. 1. Charleston: S. C. Courtenay and Co. (Reprinted, Spartanburg, S.C.: The Reprint Co., 1960.)   (16)

Longe, Alexander. See no. 48.

[207]   Lounsbury, Floyd G. 1961. "Iroquois-Cherokee Linguistic Relations." In *Symposium on Cherokee and Iroquois Culture*, eds. William N. Fenton and John Gulick, Smithsonian Institution, *Bureau*

*of American Ethnology Bulletin* 180, pp. 11-18. Washington, D.C.: U.S. Government Printing Office. (7, 28)

[208] Lumpkin, Wilson. 1907. *The Removal of the Cherokee Indians from Georgia.* 2 vols. New York: Dodd, Mead and Co. (Reprinted, New York: Arno Press, 1969.) (20)

[209]* Malone, Henry T. 1956. *Cherokees of the Old South: A People in Transition.* Athens: University of Georgia Press. (17)

[210] Martin, Robert G., Jr., 1947. "The Cherokee Phoenix: Pioneer of Indian Journalism." *Chronicles of Oklahoma* 25:102-18. (31)

[211] McClary, Ben Harris. 1962. "Nancy Ward: The Last Beloved Woman of the Cherokees." *Tennessee Historical Quarterly* 21:352-64. (41)

[212] McCoy, George and H. F. Fulling. 1961. *History of the Stomp Dance or "Sacred Fire" of the Cherokee Indian Nation*, ed. Marshall Walker. Blackgum, Okla.: Marshall Walker. (39)

[213] McKenney, Thomas L., and James Hall. 1933-34. *The Indian Tribes of North America: With Biographical Sketches and Anecdotes of the Principal Chiefs.* 3 vols. New ed., ed. Frederick Webb Hodge. Edinburgh: John Grant. (43)

[214] McLoughlin, William G. 1974. "Cherokee Anti-Missionary Sentiment, 1824-1828." *Ethnohistory* 21:361-370. (18)

[215] Mellon, Jr., Knox. 1973. "Christian Priber's Cherokee 'Kingdom of Paradise'." *Georgia Historical Quarterly* 57:319-31. (13)

[216] Meredith, Howard L., and Virginia E. Milam. 1975. "A Cherokee Vision of Eloh." *The Indian Historian* 8(4):19-23. (36)

[217] Meriwether, Colyer, ed. 1904-5. "Gen. Joseph Martin and the Cherokees." *Southern History Association Publications* 8:443-450; 9:27-41. (16)

[218] * Milling, Chapman J. 1969. *Red Carolinians*. 2nd. ed. Columbia, S.C.: University of South Carolina Press. ( 9)

[219] Moffitt, James W. 1940. "Early Baptist Missionary Work Among the Cherokees." *East Tennessee Historical Society's Publications* 12:16-27. (18)

[220] Mooney, James. 1889. "Evolution in Cherokee Personal Names." *American Anthropologist*, old series, 2:61-62. (30)

[221] ———. 1890. "The Cherokee Ball Play." *American Anthropologist*, old series: 3:105-132. (38)

[222] ———. 1891. "The Sacred Formulas of the Cherokees." Smithsonian Institution, Bureau of Ethnology, *Seventh Annual Report, 1885-1886*, pp. 301-97. Washington, D. C.: U.S. Government Printing Office. (40)

[223] ———. 1892. "Improved Cherokee Alphabets." *American Anthropologist*, old series, 5:63-64. (31)

[224] ———. 1900. "The Cherokee River Cult." *Journal of American Folklore* 13:1-10. (36)

[225] * ———. 1900. "Myths of the Cherokees." Smithsonian Institution, Bureau of American Ethnology, *Nineteenth Annual Report, 1897-98*, Part 1, pp. 3-576. Washington, D.C.: U.S. Government Printing Office. (Reprinted, New York: Johnson Reprint Co., 1970.) (8, 25)

[226] Mooney, James and Frans M. Olbrechts. 1932. *The Swimmer Manuscript: Cherokee Sacred Formulas and Medicinal Prescriptions*. Smithsonian Institution, *Bureau of American Ethnology Bulletin* 99. Washington, D.C.: U.S. Government Printing Office. (40)

[227] Morris, John W. and Edwin C. McReynolds. 1965. *Historical Atlas of*

*Oklahoma*. Norman: University of Oklahoma Press. (22)

[228] Morton, Ohland. 1953. "Confederate Government Relations with the Five Civilized Tribes." *Chronicles of Oklahoma* 31:189-204, 299-322. (23)

[229] Moulton, Gary E. 1977. *John Ross, Cherokee Chief*. Athens: University of Georgia Press. (42)

[230] Murdock, George Peter, and Timothy J. O'Leary. 1975. *Ethnographic Bibliography of North America*. 4th ed., 5 vols. New Haven: Human Relations Area Files Press. ( 7)

[231] Myer, William Edward. 1928. "Indian Trails of the Southeast." Smithsonian Institution, Bureau of American Ethnology, *Forty-second Annual Report, 1924-25*, pp. 727-857. Washington, D.C.: U.S. Government Printing Office. (15)

[232] Nuttall, Thomas. 1905. "A Journal of Travels into the Arkansas Territory during the Year 1819, with Occasional Observations on the Manners of the Aborigines." In *Early Western Travels*, 1748-1846, ed. Reuben Gold Thwaite. Vol. 13. Cleveland: Arthur H. Clark Co. (21)

[233]   O'Donnell, James H. III. 1973. *Southern Indians in the American Revolution*. Knoxville: University of Tennessee Press. (16)

[234]   Olbrechts, Frans M. 193p. "Some Cherokee Methods of Divination." *International Congress of Americanists, Proceedings* 23:547-552. New York: The Science Press Printing Co. (36)

[235]   _____. 1931. "Cherokee Belief and Practice with Regard to Childbirth." *Anthropos* 26:17-33. (40)

[236]   _____. 1931. "Two Cherokee Texts." *International Journal of American Linguistics* 6:179-184. (29)

[237] * Olds, Fred A. 1916-17. "The Cherokee Indian School." *The Redman* 9:85-90; 125-30; 212-16. (27)

[238] * Oswalt, Wendell H. 1973. "The Eastern Cherokee: Farmers of the Southeast." In *This Land Was Theirs: A Study of the North American Indian*, by Wendell H. Oswalt, 2nd ed. rev., pp. 500-527. New York: John Wiley. (27)

[239]   Otis, D. S. 1973. *The Dawes Act and the Allotment of Indian Land*, ed. Francis Paul Prucha. Norman: University of Oklahoma Press. (24)

[240] Owen, Mrs. Narcissa (Chisholm). 1907. *Memoirs of Narcissa Owen, 1831-1907.* Washington: Privately printed. (42)

[241] Peacock, Mary T. 1965. "Methodist Mission Work Among the Cherokee Indians Before the Removal." *Methodist History* 3(3):20-29. (18)

[242] * Peithman, Irvin M. 1964. *Red Men of Fire: A History of Cherokee Indians.* Springfield, Ill.: Charles Thomas. ( 9)

[243] Perdue, Theda. 1976. "People Without a Place: Aboriginal Cherokee Bondage." *The Indian Historian* 9(3)31-37. (18)

[244] Phelps, David Sutton, ed. 1974. *Anthropological Bibliography of North Carolina.* North Carolina Archaeological Council Publication 1. Raleigh: Division of Archives and History, North Carolina Department of Cultural Resources. ( 7)

[245] Pickens, A. L. 1943. "A Comparison of Cherokee and Pioneer Bird-Nomenclature." *Southern Folklore Quarterly* 7:213-21. (32)

[246] Pickett, Albert J. 1962. *History of Alabama and Incidentally of Georgia and Mississippi from the Earliest Period.* Bir-

mingham: Birmingham Book and
Magazine Co. (16)

[247] * Pierce, Earl Boyd and Rennard Strickland. 1973. *The Cherokee People*. Phoenix: Indian Tribal Series. ( 9)

[248] Pilling, James C. 1888. *Bibliography of the Iroquoian Languages*. Smithsonian Institution, *Bureau of Ethnology Bulletin* 6. Washington, D.C.: U.S. Government Printing Office. (29)

[249] Prucha, Francis Paul. 1962. *American Indian Policy in the Formative Years: The Indian Trade and Intercourse Acts, 1790-1834*. Cambridge: Harvard University Press. (20)

[250] ———. 1977. *A Bibliographical Guide to the History of Indian-White Relations in the United States*. Chicago: University of Chicago Press. ( 7)

[251] * Purrington, Burton L. ed. 1975. *New Perspectives on the Cherokees*. Special Cherokee Issue, *Appalachian Journal* 2:250-356. (28)

[252] Putnam, Albigence Waldo. 1859. *History of Middle Tennessee, or Life and Times of Gen. James Robertson*. Nashville: Printed for the Author. (Reprinted,

with introduction by Stanley F. Horn and index by Hugh and Cornelia Walker, Knoxville: University of Tennessee Press, 1971.) (16)

[253] Ramsey, James Gettys McGready. 1853. *Annals of Tennessee to the End of the 18th Century: comprising Its Settlement as the Watauga Association, from 1769 to 1777; a Part of North-Carolina, from 1777 to 1784; the State of Franklin, from 1784 to 1788; a Part of North-Carolina, from 1788 to 1790; the Territory of the U. States, South of the Ohio, from 1790 to 1796; the State of Tennessee, from 1796 to 1800.* Charleston, S.C.: Walker and James. (Reprinted, Kingsport, Tenn.: Kingsport Press, 1926; Knoxville: East Tennessee Historical Society, 1967. New York: Arno Press, 1971.) (16)

[254] * Randolph, J. Ralph. 1973. *British Travelers Among the Southern Indians, 1660-1763.* Norman: University of Oklahoma Press. (14)

[255] Reagan, John H. 1897. "The Expulsion of the Cherokees from East Texas." *Quarterly of the Texas State Historical Association* 1:38-46. (21)

[256] Reid, John Phillip. 1970. *A Law of*

*Blood: The Primitive Law of the Cherokee Nation.* New York: New York University Press. (35)

[257] Rights, Douglas L. 1931. "The Trading Path to the Indians." *North Carolina Historical Review* 3:403-26. (9, 12)

[258] * _____. 1957. *The American Indian in North Carolina*, 2nd ed. Winston-Salem, N.C.: John F. Blair. ( 9)

[259] Robinson, W. Stitt. 1964. "Virginia and the Cherokees: Indian Policy from Spotswood to Dinwiddie." In *The Old Dominion: Essays for Thomas Perkins Abernathy*, ed. D. B. Rutnam, pp. 21-40. Charlottesville: University Press of Virginia. (14)

[260] Rogin, Michael Paul. 1975. *Fathers and Children: Andrew Jackson and the Subjugation of the American Indians.* New York: Alfred A. Knopf. (20)

[261] Ross, William P. 1893. *The Life and Times of Hon. William P. Ross*, ed. Mrs. William P. Ross. Fort Smith, Ark.: Weldon and Williams. (42)

[262] Rothrock, Mary U. 1929. "Carolina Traders Among the Overhill Cherokees, 1690-1760." *East Tennessee Historical Society's Publications* 1: 3-18. (12)

[263]　　Rouse, Irving, and John M. Goggin, eds. 1947. *An Anthropological Bibliography of the Eastern Seaboard. Eastern States Archaeological Federation Research Publication* No. 1. New Haven: Eastern States Archaeological Federation.　　( 7)

[264]　　Royce, Charles C. 1887. "The Cherokee Nation of Indians: A Narrative of their Official Relations with the Colonial and Federal Governments." Smithsonian Institution. Bureau of Ethnology. *Fifth Annual Report, 1833-84*, pp. 121-378. Washington, D.C.: U.S. Government Printing Office. (Reprinted, Chicago: Aldine Publishing Co., 1975.)　　( 9)

[265] *　Ruskin, Gertrude M. 1963. *John Ross, Chief of an Eagle Race*. John Ross House Association. Privately Printed.　　(42)

[266]　　Russell, Mattie U. 1974. "Devil in the Smokies: The White Man's Nature and the Indian's Fate." *South Atlantic Quarterly* 73:53-69.　　(27)

[267]　　Rutland, Robert A. 1949-50. "Political Background of the Cherokee Treaty of New Echota." *Chronicles of Oklahoma* 27:389-406.　　(20)

[268]　　Satz, Ronald N. 1975. *American Indian*

*Policy in the Jacksonian Era*. Lincoln: University of Nebraska Press. (20)

[269] Schwarze, Edmund. 1923. *History of the Moravian Missions Among Southern Indian Tribes of the United States. Transactions of the Moravian Historical Society*, Special Series, Vol. 1. Bethlehem, Pa.: Times Publishing Co. (17)

[270] Sears, William H. 1955. "Creek and Cherokee Culture in the 18th Century." *American Antiquity* 21:143-49. (10)

[271] Setzler, Frank M. and Jesse D. Jennings. 1941. *Peachtree Mound and Village Site, Cherokee County, North Carolina*. Smithsonian Institution, *Bureau of American Ethnology Bulletin* 131. Washington, D.C.: U.S. Government Printing Office. (10)

[272] * Silverberg, Robert. 1968. *Mound Builders of Ancient America: The Archaeology of a Myth*. Greenwich, Conn.: New York Graphic Society. (10)

[273] Skinner, Alanson B. 1910. "Cherokee Collection." in R. H. Lowie (ed), "Notes Concerning New Collections." *Anthropological Papers of the American Museum of Natural History*: 4, pt. 2, pp. 284-289. New York: The Trustees. (33)

[274] * Spade, Watt and Willard Walker. 1966. *Cherokee Stories*. Middletown, Conn.: Laboratory of Anthropology, Wesleyan University. (37)

[275] Speck, Frank G. 1920. "Decorative Art and Basketry of the Cherokee." *Bulletin of the Public Museum of the City of Milwaukee* 2, pp. 53-86. Milwaukee, Wisc.: The Trustees. (33)

[276] _____. 1926. "Some Eastern Cherokee Texts." *International Journal of American Linguistics* 4:111-13. (29)

[277] _____. 1938. "The Cane Blowgun in Catawba and Southeastern Ethnology." *American Anthropologist* 40:198-204. (33)

[278] _____. 1941. *Gourds of the Southeastern Indians; A Prolegomenon on the Lagenaria Gourd in the Culture of the Southeastern Indians*. Boston: New England Gourd Society. (33)

[279] _____. 1946. "Ethnoherpetology of the Catawba and Cherokee Indians." *Journal of the Washington Academy of Sciences* 36:355-60. (32)

[280] _____. 1950. *Concerning Iconology and the Masking Complex in Eastern North America*. University Museum Bulletin 15:6-57. Philadelphia. (38)

[281]   Speck, Frank G., and Leonard Broom. 1951. *Cherokee Dance and Drama*. Berkeley: University of California Press.   (35, 39)

[282]   Speck, Frank G. and C. E. Schaeffer. 1945. "The Mutual-Aid and Volunteer Company of the Eastern Cherokee: as Recorded in a Book of Minutes in the Sequoyah Syllabary, compared with Mutual-Aid Societies of the Northern Iroquois." *Journal of the Washington Academy of Sciences* 35:169-79.   (34)

[283]   Spoehr, Alexander. 1947. *Changing Kinship Systems. A Study in the Acculturation of the Creeks, Cherokee, and Choctaw*. Field Museum, Anthropological Series, 33:153-235.   (34)

[284] * Starkey, Marion L. 1946. *The Cherokee Nation*. New York: Alfred A. Knopf. (Reprinted, New York: Russell and Russell, 1972.)   (9, 18)

[285]   _____. 1921. *History of the Cherokee Indians and their Legends and Folklore*. Oklahoma City: Warden Company. (Reprinted, eds. Jack Gregory and Rennard Strickland, Fayetteville, Ark.: Indian Heritage Association, 1967 and New York: Kraus Reprint, 1969.)   (22)

[286] * Starr, Frederick. 1899. *American Indians*. Boston: D.C. Heath and Co. (27)

[287] Strange, Robert. 1960. *Eoneguski, or The Cherokee Chief 1839*. Facsimile ed., forward by Richard Walser. Charlotte, N.C.: McNally. (43)

[288] Strickland, Rennard. 1970. "Christian Gottlieb Priber: Utopian Precursor of the Cherokee Government." *Chronicles of Oklahoma* 48:264-79. (13)

[289] ———. 1975. *Fire and the Spirits: Cherokee Law from Clan to Court*. Norman: University of Oklahoma Press. (5, 35)

[290] Suddeth, Ruth Elgin. 1956. "The Myths of the Cherokees." *The Georgia Review* 10:84-91. (37)

[291] Swanton, John Reed. 1946. *The Indians of the Southeastern United States*, Smithsonian Institution, *Bureau of American Ethnology Bulletin* 137. Washington, D.C.: U.S. Government Printing Office. (6)

[292] Taylor, Lydia Averill. 1940. *Plants Used as Curatives by Certain Southeastern Tribes*. Cambridge: Harvard University Botanical Museum. (32)

[293] Thomas, Robert K. 1961. "The Redbird Smith Movement." In *Symposium on*

*Cherokee and Iroquois Culture*, eds. William N. Fenton and John Gulick, Smithsonian Institution, *Bureau of American Ethnology Bulletin* 180, pp. 159-66. Washington, D.C.: U.S. Government Printing Office (24, 39)

[294] _____. 1967. "The Role of the Church in Indian Adjustment." *Kansas Journal of Sociology* 3:20-28. (25)

[295] Thomas, Robert K. and Albert L. Wahrhaftig. 1971. "Indians, Hillbillies, and the 'Education Problem'." In *Anthropological Perspectives on Education*, eds. Murray Wax, Stanley Diamond and Fred O. Gearing, pp. 230-51. New York: Basic Books, Inc. (25)

[296] Traveller Bird. 1971. *Tell Them They Lie: The Sequoyah Myth*. Los Angeles: Westernlore Publishers. (30)

[297] Travis, V. A. 1926. "Life in the Cherokee Nation a Decade after the Civil War." *Chronicles of Oklahoma* 4:16-30.

[298] * Ulmer, Mary, and Samuel E. Beck. eds. 1951. *To Make My Bread: Preparing Cherokee Foods*. Cherokee, N.C.: Museum of the Cherokee Indian. (32)

[299] * Van Every, Dale. 1966. *Disinherited: The Lost Birthright of the American Indian*. New York: William Morrow. (21)

[300] Vassar, Rena, ed. 1961. "Some Short Remarkes on the Indian Trade in the Charikees and in the Managment Therof since the Year 1717." *Ethnohistory* 8:401-23. (12)

[301] Wahrhaftig, Albert L. 1966. "Community and the Caretakers." *New University Thought* 4(4):54-76. (25)

[302] _____. 1968. "The Tribal Cherokee Population of Eastern Oklahoma." *Current Anthropology* 9:510-18. (25)

[303] _____. 1970. *The Social and Economic Characteristics of the Tribal Cherokee Population of Eastern Oklahoma; Report of a Survey of Four Cherokee Settlements in the Cherokee Nation. American Anthropological Association Anthropological Studies* 5. (25)

[304] _____. 1975. "Institution Building Among Oklahoma's Traditional Cherokees." In *Four Centuries of Southern Indians*, ed. Charles M. Hudson, pp. 132-47. Athens: University of Georgia Press. (25)

[305] _____. 1975. "More Than Mere Work: The Subsistence System of Oklahoma's Cherokee Indians." *Appalachia Journal* 2:327-331. (25)

[306] Wahrhaftig, Albert L. and Jane Lukens-Wahrhaftig. 1977. "The Thrice

Powerless: Cherokee Indians in Oklahoma." In *The Anthropology of Power*, eds. Raymond D. Fogelson and Richard N. Adams, pp. 225-36. New York: Academic Press. (34)

[307] Wahrhaftig, Albert L. and Robert K. Thomas. 1968. "Renaissance and Repression: The Oklahoma Cherokee." *Trans-action* 6(4):42-48. (25)

[308] * Walker, Robert Sparks. 1931. *Torchlights to the Cherokees: The Brainerd Mission*. New York: The Macmillan Co. (18)

[309] Walker, Willard. 1969. "Notes on Native Writing Systems and the Design of Native Literacy Programs." *Anthropological Linguistics* 11:148-66. (31)

[310] _____. 1975. "Cherokee." In *Studies in Southeastern Indian Languages*, ed. James M. Crawford, pp. 189-236. Athens: University of Georgia Press. (29)

[311] Wardell, Morris L. 1938. *A Political History of the Cherokee Nation, 1838-1907*. Norman: University of Oklahoma Press. (22)

[312] Warren, Hanna R. 1967. "Reconstruction in the Cherokee Nation." *Chronicles of Oklahoma* 45:180-189. (24)

[313]   Washburn, Cephas. 1869. *Reminiscences of the Indians*. Richmond, Va.: Presbyterian Committee of Publication. (Reprinted, New York: Johnson Reprint, 1971.) (23)

[314]   _____. 1910. Cherokees "West," 1794 to 1893 Claremore, Okla.: Emmet Starr, Publisher. (21)

[315]   Washburn, Wilcomb E. 1975. *The Assault on Indian Tribalism: The General Allotment Law (Dawes Act) of 1887*. Philadelphia: J. B. Lippincott. (24)

[316] * Wax, Murray. 1971. *Indian Americans: Unity and Diversity*. Englewood Cliffs, N.J.: Prentice-Hall. (25)

[317]   Whitaker, A. P. 1927. "Spain and the Cherokee Indians, 1783-1798." *North Carolina Historical Review* 4:252-69. (16)

[318]   White, John K. 1962. "On the Revival of Printing in the Cherokee Language." *Current Anthropology* 3:511-14. (31)

[319]   White, Max E. 1975. "Contemporary Usage of Native Plant Foods by the Eastern Cherokee." *Appalachian Journal* 2:323-26. (32)

[320]   White, Robert C. 1973. *Cherokee Indian Removal from the Lower Hiwassee Valley*.

Cleveland: Cleveland State Community College. (21)

[321] Wilburn, Hiram C. 1950. "Nununyi, the Kituhwas, or Mountain Indians and the State of North Carolina." *Southern Indian Studies* 2:54-64. (28)

[322] * ———. 1951. *Chief Junaluska*. Asheville, N.C.: Stephens Press. (42)

[323] ———. 1952. "Judaculla Place-Names and the Judaculla Tales." *Southern Indian Studies* 4:23-26. (11)

[324] ———. 1952. "Judaculla Rock." *Southern Indian Studies* 4:19-22. (11)

[325] ———. 1959. "The Cherokee Indians of Jackson County, North Carolina." *Southern Indian Studies* 11:20-22. (28)

[326] * Wilkins, Thurman. 1970. *Cherokee Tragedy: The Story of the Ridge Family and the Decimation of a People*. New York: Macmillan. (20, 42)

[327] Williams, Samuel Cole, ed. 1927. *Lieutenant Henry Timberlake: Memoirs, 1756-1765*. Johnson City, Tenn.: The Watauga Press. (12)

[328] ———. ed. 1928. *Early Travels in the Tennessee Country, 1540-1800*. Johnson City, Tenn.: The Watauga Press. (13, 18)

[329] ———. 1931. "An Account of the Presbyterian Mission to the Cherokee, 1757-1759." *Tennessee Historical Magazine*, series 2, 1:125-38. (13)

[330] * ———. 1937. *Dawn of Tennessee Valley and Tennessee History*. Johnson City, Tenn.: The Watauga Press. (14)

[331] ———. 1944. *Tennessee During the Revolutionary War*. Nashville: The Tennessee Historical Commission. (16)

[332] Willis, William S., Jr., 1963. "Patrilineal Institutions in Southeastern North America." *Ethnohistory* 10:250-69. (34)

[333] Wilms, Douglas C. 1974. "Cherokee Settlement Patterns in Nineteenth Century Georgia." *Southeastern Geographer* 14:46-53. (34)

[334] Winkler, Ernest William. 1903. "The Cherokee Indians in Texas." *Quarterly of the Texas State Historical Association* 7:95-165. (21)

[335] Witthoft, John. 1946. "Bird Lore of the Eastern Cherokee." *Journal of the Washington Academy of Sciences* 36:372-84. (32)

[336] ———. 1946. "The Green Corn Medicine and the Green Corn Festival."

*Journal of the Washington Academy of Sciences* 36:213-19. (39)

[337] * _____. 1946. "Some Eastern Cherokee Bird Stories." *Journal of the Washington Academy of Sciences* 36:177–80. (37)

[338] _____. 1947. "An Early Cherokee Ethnobotanical Note." *Journal of the Washington Academy of Sciences* 37:73-75. (32)

[339] _____. 1947. "Notes on a Cherokee Migration Story." *Journal of the Washington Academy of Sciences* 37:304-05. (37)

[340] _____. 1948. "Will West Long, Cherokee Informant." *American Anthropologist* 50:355-59. (43)

[341] _____. 1949. "Green Corn Ceremonialism in the Eastern Woodlands." *Occasional Contributions from the Museum of Anthropology of the University of Michigan* no. 13. (38)

[342] _____. 1949. "Stone Pipes of the Historic Cherokees." *Southern Indian Studies* 1:43-62. (33, 38)

[343] _____. 1961. "Eastern Woodland Community Typology and Acculturation." in *Symposium on Cherokee and Iro-*